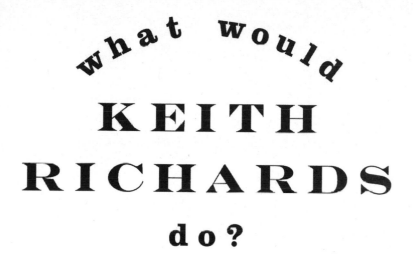

what would
KEITH
RICHARDS
do?

what would
KEITH
RICHARDS
do?

DAILY AFFIRMATIONS
FROM A
ROCK 'N' ROLL SURVIVOR

JESSICA PALLINGTON WEST

BLOOMSBURY
NEW YORK · BERLIN · LONDON

This work is not endorsed, sponsored,
or authorized by Keith Richards.

Published by Bloomsbury USA, New York

Keith's mum's shepherd's pie recipe reproduced by permission from Wendy
Diamond, *A Musical Feast: Recipes from over 100 of the World's Most Famous Musical
Artists,* (New York: Global Liasons, Incorporated, 1995), 83.

All papers used by Bloomsbury USA are natural, recyclable products made from
wood grown in well-managed forests. The manufacturing processes conform to the
environmental regulations of the country of origin.

Library of Congress Cataloging-in-Publication Data

Richards, Keith, 1943–
What would Keith Richards do?: daily affirmations from a rock and roll survivor/
[collected by] Jessica Pallington West. —1st U.S. ed.
p. cm.
Includes bibliographical references.
ISBN-13: 978-1-59691-614-2
ISBN-10: 1-59691-614-1
1. Richards, Keith, 1943—Quotations. I. West, Jessica Pallington. II. Title.

ML420. R515A25, 2009
782. 42166092—dc22
2008048220

First U.S. edition 2009

1 3 5 7 9 10 8 6 4 2

Design by Lauren Monchik
Typeset by Hewer Text UK Ltd, Edinburgh
Printed in the United States of America by Quebecor World Fairfield

By the same author

Lipstick

For the two Keiths

"I'll see my name in bookshops, and I'll think, 'What am I doing here?' ... It's like knowing everybody."

— *KEITH RICHARDS: IN HIS OWN WORDS*, 1992

"If Keith Richards didn't exist, Rock 'n' Roll would have to invent him."

— *CHATELAINE* MAGAZINE

TABLE OF CONTENTS

INTRODUCTION

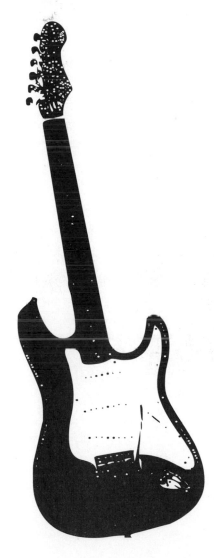

Somehow he's managed to survive.

But it hasn't been easy:

Beaten up every day coming home from school. A move to the wrong side of town. A little addiction to heroin. Arrested. Arrested again. Court. Court again. Accused of being Satan's right-hand man. A night in jail. A broken finger. Three broken ribs. A broken nose. A punctured lung. A crashed car. Another crashed car. Brain surgery. Cold turkey. Cold turkey again. Attacked by a fan. Electrocuted on stage, saved by a pair of Hush Puppies. Knocked unconscious by flying garbage. Disowned by father. Turned in to police by a company insider. Bilked out of millions by a sleazy manager. The loss of a child. The loss of a friend. The loss of another friend. Blamed for a friend's death. Framed. Stoned. Did I mention getting arrested? Another crashed car. The house is broken into by cops. The house is broken into by vandals. The house goes up in flames. The other house goes up in flames. Hauled into court. Acquitted, there's a celebration party at a hotel, and the hotel room is accidentally set on fire. The bed goes up in flames. A hit song is unwittingly stolen from another artist. The recording studio goes up in flames. The evil twin misbehaves. The evil twin gets knighted.

What does all this add up to?

Keith Richards.

And this is only a fraction of the story, just a snip off the timeline of trouble.

Keith's ability to survive has not just been a matter of having genes of steel. Much of it comes out of his uniquely "Keef" way of looking at life—an attitude and vision that he's fine-tuned over the years like a guitar. There's a philosopher's aesthetic in how he expresses it, a uniquely Keith quality. It's the no-nonsense, salt-of-the-earth, been-there-done-that wisdom of a survivor.

The Tao of Keith is one of humanity, of seeing with clarity, and looking at the bigger picture of history and culture. There is a respect for the mystical and a reverence for the creative. It's bullshit-free, human, and down to earth. Bemused, brave, and kind.

Imagine Abraham Lincoln with a skull ring, an earring, and a scarf. A little bit Ben Franklin and a little bit Billy the Kid. He's a wise statesman mixed with back-alley tough, Buddha, and pirate. And what's specifically unique about Keith is that he's the first to take rock 'n' roll as far as it can go. He's rock 'n' roll matured, a visionary and a rogue: a prophet minstrel who's walked through fire. Rock's first wise man is a symbol of survival, one knockdown after another. With Keith, we have a new form of guru: a modern, street-wise, urban guru.

As a symbol of staying power, the words, wisdom, and philosophy of Keith can be used as an example to improve your own life in times of confusion. There's a whole doctrine that has grown up around Keith. It comes down to learning a set of Keith Richards Commandments—basic tenets and rules to follow. Through them, it's quite possible that Keith Richards can save your life. Or at least save your ass.

The principles of Keithism come directly from his own words: Imparting wisdom through the numerous interviews he's given along the way like a rock 'n' roll Socrates holding court, Keith has talked about his run-ins with the law, his falling into and then out of trouble, defying death, and bouncing back. It's a fairly simple philosophy to follow—no fancy tricks. The principles are down-home and plainspoken.

The tenets of this way of life are from the same side of town as the Ten Commandments. But remember, they're coming from Keith Richards, the avatar of excess. And so the number of commandments is more than just *ten*.

Here are the Twenty-six Ten Commandments of Keith Richards.

Forget that other book about a Secret that will save you. Here are twenty-six secrets: rule-book tenets handed down not from Mount Sinai, but from Mount Been-There-Done-It, where the golden calf sings the blues and the Commandments are written out on unrolled cigarettes.

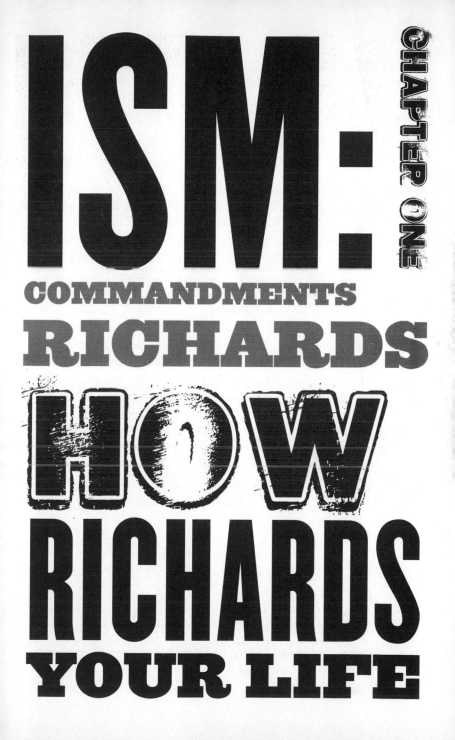

ISM: CHAPTER ONE

COMMANDMENTS

RICHARDS

HOW

RICHARDS

YOUR LIFE

1. KNOW YOURSELF.

"To me, the main thing about living on this planet is to know who the hell you are and to be real about it. That's the reason I'm still alive ... I've lived my life my own way, and I'm here because I've taken the trouble to find out who I am."

Above all, this is the golden rule of Keithism: know yourself. From this doctrine, all else will fall into place.

And, along with knowing yourself, know your limits. Know how much you can take on. Know how much you can take in.

Let this knowledge come from listening.

We are all a work of music—listen to the song. You might have to put the earplugs in every now and then, but that's okay.

Once you have a sense of what your limitations are—how much, where, and when—it's not so daunting to live with yourself. And you don't need to fight so hard against it. If you are a slower person, so be it. If you have a quick temper, so be it again. If you can take only sixty-four steps a day, or can't eat in crowds, or can't resist the urge to dye your hair purple: fine. But if you break into hives every time your scalp feels the burn of the lavender dye: take heed. Accept your qualities and your limitations. Other people can tell you who you are, and who they think you are, but in the end, only you really know.

"You've seen it all, done it all. You've survived. That's the trick, isn't it? To survive?"—Jack Sparrow, played by Johnny Depp, in Pirates of the Caribbean

"It's not just about living forever, Jackie. The trick is living with yourself forever."—Captain Teague, Sparrow's father, played by Keith Richards

"He was one of the people I admired for what he's done and how he's handled it. Forty-whatever years of being this god. And he's just cool."—Johnny Depp, talking about how he based his rendition of Jack Sparrow on Keith

You can imitate all you want, but you always come back home to yourself. You can put on a Halloween costume, but it only covers up so much. You can run, but you can't hide. At the end of the marathon, *you* are still there. The buck stops with you. Always follow what you know is right—morally, ethically, aesthetically.

2. WE ARE ALL THE SAME UNDER THE SKIN.
"The skull—it has nothing to do with bravado and surface bullshit ... Beauty is skin-deep. This is what we are all like under the flesh, brother. Take off the hair, pull off the skin, you're looking at the I and I."

Look at a photo of Keith Richards, and, besides the lit cigarette, you'll always see two things: the handcuff bracelet and the skull ring. Both are always there, as reminders. With the handcuff, it is a reminder that freedom is something not to be taken for granted. With the skull ring: it's that we're all the same underneath the skin. And that there is no time for bullshit. We're all the same.

This concept has been expressed through time by great minds in both high art and low. To take a view from the low road: there's an old episode of the TV show *The Brady Bunch,* in which an authority-shy Marcia can't pass her driving test unless she envisions the instructor in his T-shirt and boxers. The *Brady Bunch* lesson and secret learned is this: When you're intimidated by someone, imagine them in their underwear. It works. The intimidation goes up in smoke. The skull is the same basic concept of the *Brady Bunch* underpants—just a little more chilling. But the message, at bottom, isn't to say, "Screw you." It's to inspire compassion. As Keith's soul-brother Plato wrote: "Be kind, for everyone you meet is fighting a hard battle." As Keith has said, "Skulls remind us that underneath it all, we are all the same."

3. THERE ARE NO SECRETS.
"I've got nothing to hide. Nothing's a state secret with me."

It's not a bad rule to live by. There's a similar principle in Alcoholics Anonymous: "You're only as sick as your secrets." And you've heard this well-known maxim: "The truth will set you free." Or, from Mark Twain: "If you tell the truth, you don't have to remember anything." Truth is stranger than fiction, and it's far more interesting. Truth is a fine wine; lies are Boone's Farm. Why not enjoy the best? Life is too short.

Keith has always maintained that if you want to look into his windows, he'll pull the curtain farther open for you so you can get a better view.

"Anything you put on your front page, I can top it. Because I'll give you the real lowdown, which is far more interesting ... I don't want anybody to think it's worth snooping around in my backyard thinking they're gonna pick up anything that they wouldn't learn by asking me."

Be the aggressor. When you're completely candid, nobody can snoop in your closet.

"There's nothing that can be said about me that everybody doesn't know. You can't have a worse reputation than mine. I realized in the seventies that I had no reason to lie, that everyone was going to believe far worse anyway. I had nothing left to cover up ... There's nothing worth lying about."

Don't be afraid of inquiry. As much as you can, let any subject be up for discussion. Bring it on, and take it on. You can decide whether or not you want to answer it, but its okay for them to ask.

There's just one exception: anything having to do with Elton John. Leave that one alone. Anything else. Just not Elton. That's a portal to trouble.

4. ACCEPT THE ROLLING STONES AS YOUR METAPHORICAL OVERLORD.
"There's the sun, there's the moon, there's the air we breathe, and there's the Rolling Stones."

This is a Keith favorite. And it's not merely a bloated opinion about the band he happens to play guitar for. As with many of Keith's well-traveled subjects—drugs, the self, the guitar, and, of course, Mick—the Rolling Stones is something that takes on higher metaphorical meaning when Keith starts talking. The Stones amounts to an overlord—an entity that we helped create but that has become bigger than we are.

We all have something that we are part of, whether it's a family, a community, a crowd in the street, an economy. Or our little spot in the grand picture—the world as a whole.

We are part of creating things that become Frankenstein monsters. That monster can then be one of creativity or destruction, nurturing or neglect. Shelley's monster, after all, was never inherently evil—it was only pushed into a dark corner by those who created it.

What are some other Rolling Stoneses? Offices. Corporations. Societies—the open ones and the secret ones and those trying to be utopias. Neighborhoods. Governments. Things that we refer to as some ominous "other presence"—a "them." But who makes up the "them"? Who makes up the invisible mystical force that somehow became a noun?

Recognize that you're essential to the creation and continuation of whatever your particular Rolling Stones is. You can nurture it, or keep away from it, but remember: "*It's bigger than both of us, baby*."

It is without us, but it is also within us.

Direct thyself. Create thyself.

"The Stones always have to look for the Stones in themselves."

5. THE CONSTRUCT OF THE BAND IS A MODEL FOR INTERACTION.

"Chemistry was one of those subjects in school that I was never good at … but I think it's the unknown bit—the mysterious spark—that does it. It's the same with the Stones. I mean, line 'em up against a wall, and they're the most unlikely good rock 'n' roll band that you could find! … There's something to be said for a certain chemistry between people that makes for a certain kind of music."

It has repeatedly been noted about the Stones that, just as with the Beat-les, much of their success and magic came down to the right combination of people. Just the right chemical combination. Ron Wood put his two cents in here as well: "Individually, we hardly make an impression, but together we have a power which is beyond us." The sum of the separate personalities when brought together—as well as the instruments—creates a symphony, a song. The unit of a band is a conglomeration of balancing personalities and instruments. It is stronger as a whole.

In living life the Keith Richards way, we accept different personalities and styles as separate entities that are necessary to work together. They all have a need and a purpose. Even Mick. The members of the band are "other selves." They all work in harmony, creating one sound.

Of course, some bands are better than others. And as much as you can, listen closely to the music and decipher which are the good and bad bands. Veer toward the good, steer away from the bad. While good music is health for the soul, crappy music can destroy it. Or cause insanity.

If the other band members look as if they have to stand in front of the mirror to practice spitting, say no. Some quick tips on bad bands: Anything where there's a lot of posing going on, run. In this realm, according to Keith: David Bowie, Beck, Duran Duran. Or anyone who needs a shave, like George Michael. Or that needs a good ten more years of growing up before you can look at it without rolling your eyes, like Oasis. And anything that has even a touch of

Elton John in it—*run like the goddamn wind*. Run as if the candles in the wind had fallen off their holders and were about to set the place on fire. Run as if Satan himself were after you.

Good bands: AC/DC. Motorhead. Anything *real* that has an authentic "human touch." Little Richard, Elvis, Buddy Holly. There should be no doubt that the singer means what he's saying.

Overkill of saxophones: Protect your loved ones from this. Sixteen guitars: They're faking it. The absence of a drummer: suspect. If it has no heartbeat, it's not alive. And stay away from Eric Clapton. You'll end up as Eric Clapton and the Rolling Stones. You need a *band*.

And if the band you're with isn't necessarily the best, remember one of Keith's main credos: "There's always the future." Every gig leads forward and, hopefully, to something better.

While we must ultimately know ourselves and be true to ourselves, know that it is through the larger construct of the group that the real magic can happen. It is through the *group* that the most beautiful things, and art, can come about:

"Rock 'n' roll is really about interaction ... It's about the interesting tension and communication going on between one guy and another ... You can't find it on any meter in the studio. Songs, to me, come through osmosis. All the best songs are basically beautiful accidents."

6. ACCEPT (OR AT LEAST TOLERATE) YOUR INNER AND OUTER MICK.
"Mick's rock. I'm roll."

Dual nature? Evil twin? We've all got one. No use fighting it. If you come at your evil twin with a pillow in the middle of the night, he will rise like a ghost from the mattress. He will haunt your dreams.

Might as well get used to him.

And while you're getting used to him, put that evil twin to work for you. Or work with him.

Mick Jagger and Keith Richards are two sides of a set of Siamese twins. Attached, inseparable. But different. Keith is the evil twin to Mick, and Mick is the evil twin to Keith.

But there is an art to keeping that evil twin in check. In Keithism, it's called Accepting Your Inner and Outer Mick.

Every time Keith Richards sits down and starts talking, the subject of Mick Jagger inevitably comes up, and when it does, Mick becomes a metaphor for the second self. And while that second half can be frustrating and annoying, it is there for a reason. It is a counterbalance to your true self. The one you've come to know through the first tenet. It's a moon for the sun. A dark crayon for a light one.

Sometimes the evil twin lives inside of you, which isn't so bad, since you can keep an eye on it. But when it is its own creature, wandering about in the form of another person, it can be a little hard. It becomes the Outer Mick versus the Inner Mick. Still, they can both be handled by the same formula.

There are five steps to accepting the Inner or Outer Mick: 1) Identifying him, 2) Understanding the creature, 3) Embracing him as such, 4) Helping to bring out the best that is in him, and 5) Learning from him.

A yin exists for its yang. Rock exists for roll.

Without a Keith there would be no Mick, and vice versa. We have this within ourselves and within the worlds we live in.

7. NURTURE YOUR INNER CHARLIE.
"If only Mozart had had a really good drummer ..."

The near-perfect person, in Keith's eyes, has always been Charlie Watts. Watts is the ultimate individualist, removed from the mainstream, a little shy, eccentric, humble. Has his own specific beat. The backbone to both the group and the individual is the drummer. Solidify a moral, modest, ethical, and pretention-free backbone, and you're in good shape. From a solid drummer, all else falls into place. Find the Rolling Stones within yourself, but be sure that the drummer is strong and not a poseur.

"... And if only Bach had a really good drummer ... If only ..."

8. ACCEPT YOUR ADDICTIONS, VIEW THEM WITH HUMOR, AND LEAVE OFF THE GUILT.
"I don't like to regret heroin because I learned a lot from it. It is something I went through and dealt with. I'd regret it if I hadn't dealt with it."

There is an old saying: "An opinion is like an asshole. Everybody's got one." Another truth: Addiction is like an asshole. Everyone's got one of these as well. Or two. Or three. It's easy to judge the other guy when the addiction he's got is different from your own, but once you try his on for size, or vice versa, then you begin to understand. As Rousseau wrote: "We pity in others only those evils which we ourselves have experienced."

But in the world of Keith, the key is not to eliminate our addictions but to survive them. And these are the keys:

1) Accept your addiction and know that the experience of it has made you who you are and has enhanced you individually.
2) Have a sense of humor toward your own darkness.
3) Screw the guilt.

Number three is what bangs it all into place.

And ultimately, what is important is *where you come out on the other side*. The real thing is facing the problem, dealing with it, and working it out.

Know, too, that addictions are not necessarily weaknesses. They are afflictions, diseases. It can be any number of things. An inability to stop sneezing. Anxiety. OCD. Depression. An intestinal system in love with diarrhea. A bum leg. They all come upon us as weakening monsters, take hold, and don't easily let go until they do. Because we can defeat them.

It is not our addictions that kill us. Not if we survive them. As

Keith said, "I've never had a problem with drugs. I've only had a problem with policemen."

We all have our metaphorical heroin problem. Maybe we all have our metaphorical policemen too.

9. MAKE USE OF THE MUSIC AROUND YOU, YOUR ANTENNA, AND YOUR INNER GUITAR.

"I don't think I write the songs; I'm an antenna. Actually, you receive the songs ... You just sit around a piano or pick up a guitar, and for me, after about ten or fifteen minutes, something that I haven't heard before starts to come out, and then I just sort of put it into shape and then I transmit it, you know."

Keith's instrument of choice, the guitar, is more than wood and strings. The instrument connects with an inner antenna and then picks up waves from the world around it, transforming those waves into something new.

"I look at that guitar sometimes and think, there's only six strings and twelve frets, man. But the more you play it, the more things come out of it ... Things arrive in a strange order. If you can retain the mystery and turn-on of finding things out, then you can't put the goddamn thing down. It's too intriguing."

Find an instrument. An instrument can be a voice, writing, painting, woodwork, pot holders. You'd be surprised what an antenna can transmit onto a pot holder.

And then put up the antenna, and let the waves come back.

"The songs are already out there. They're there ... People think you're a songwriter, they think you wrote it, it's all yours, you are totally responsible for it. Really, you are just a medium, you just develop a facility for recognizing and picking up things and you just have to be ready to be there, like being at a séance—they just plop out of the air. Whole songs just come to you, you don't write it. I didn't do anything except to happen to have been awake when it arrived."

Channel the ether's song whether it's coming out of the wind, or the smoke elegantly wafting from the burning toaster, or the flickering bits of fire as the house, once again, goes up in flames. The beautiful accidents are waiting.

10. PUT THE ANCIENT ART OF WEAVING TO WORK.

"We had two guitars weaving around each other. We'd play these things so much that we knew both guitar parts. So when we got to the crucial point where we got it really flash, we'd suddenly switch. The lead picks up the rhythm, and the rhythm picks up the lead. It's what Ronnie and I call the ancient art of weaving. We don't even have to look at each other, almost. You can feel it."

With weaving, there is no lead or rhythm guitar. Players trade back and forth. No one takes the reins of ultimate control. This is a key metaphor for communication in any relationship, be it father-son, teacher-student, or dealer-addict.

Onstage, it's a matter of two guitars. Offstage, it's a matter of two people. Two people dancing with each other on a physical, spiritual, and musical level.

There's a democracy to it, an equality. It's a dance, and the dance ultimately teaches you to accept the individual in others, and to dance with the people around you.

"There's one guy, he's just got four arms."

"At our best, me and Ronnie make the Bayeux Tapestry onstage."

You can learn a lot from guitars. The guitar can be used as a metaphor for life—as an instrument not just for making music, but by which we can understand how to create and how to interact.

"Five strings, three notes, two fingers, and an asshole, and you've got it! You can play the darned thing. That's all it takes. What you do with it is another thing."

11. OWN THE CLASSICS.
"Everybody starts by imitating their heroes."

"The greats are the greats. You know who they are."

At age fifteen, Keith sat at the top of the stairs at his home in the government housing district and continued to replay Chuck Berry and Elvis Presley until they were a part of him. The music became a part of his inner being; it became part of his blood. He later did the same with the blues, and with Hoagy Carmichael.

From a solid foundation, a house can be built. And one that is highly original.

It doesn't matter what discipline it is that you choose: This rule is essential. It's the reason that Picasso starting out learning to draw apples that actually looked like apples.

"Apart from Chuck Berry, I can do Chuck Berry better than just about anyone. But I had to stop doing Chuck Berry and start doing Keith Richards."

12. GET OUT OF YOUR HEAD AND FEEL IT.
"This is one of Ronnie's: 'Sometimes I have the feeling that thousands of people are watching me. Am I just paranoid?' If you thought about it too much it would paralyze you."

Ronnie, aka Keith Jr., was talking about being up on stage in front of a sea of people, but it can be related to any number of day-to-day experiences. The bottom line: Overanalyzing and overthinking can do you in. Trust your intuition and your instincts. Rationality can be a means of avoidance and a cop-out. Too much analysis can cripple you.

"I've always done things on a very instinctive basis, you know. I think brains have gotten in the way of too many things."

Thinking can become like a drug. Like any drug, too much is lethal. To survive on the stage of life, just feel the music. Feel it and hear it. There is music within the activities of everyday life—whether it is riding on a train, crossing a street, or riding in an elevator. Do things. Build a house. Or if not a house, a shrine to Jimi Hendrix and a tripping room. Play a power chord. Set another house or bed on fire. Throw another car over the cliff and watch it go up in a spectacularly rich combination of flames. Get out of the head and into the body. Brains are great, but they can't eat, or reproduce, or save a woman from a burning building. Only your body can help you with that.

"I don't think onstage. I feel. Once you get up there, you're who you are. We're just feeling."

Feel the music. Go with it.

And *touch*. Ever notice how much these guys in the Stones touch each other? It's a visceral connection. Touch what is close to you and what you love. Touch the people you know. If there are no people, touch *things*. Go for all of it: craggy, hard, spiked, silken, smooth, iced over, underwater. Put your hands on things. You can always use a Band-Aid if you get hurt.

13. EVEN IF YOU HAVE TO DO IT IN SECRET, BE KIND.

Help others who are down on their luck and less fortunate.

An attitude of not giving a damn does not equate to being cruel.

Don't let Keith's bad-boy image fool you. There's more than a little romanticizing of the image going on here. This is a guy who is secretly known for a deep moral streak that verges on some serious squareness. Maybe it goes deeper than this. Maybe you don't have to give a damn to do someone a favor. Sometimes it's good for your ego. Or makes for stronger chord sequences.

As original Stones member Ian Stewart said, "I saw the old devil do good deeds on the sly." The streak of kindness goes way back. Look at this fan letter to *Tiger Beat* magazine in 1964: "I happen to know that the last time they were in town, Keith personally phoned an invalid girl who had been sick for years. After she heard his voice, the girl began to improve. Now she's almost well. Don't tell me the Stones are godless boys."

Karma is a boomerang. One act of kindness came back in a whamming boomerang in Canada, during Keith's drug trial.

There was a blind teenager from Toronto who continued to show up at Stones concerts, and Keith was the one who looked after her, who made sure that she was taken care of and driven home. After all, as Keith said, "God knows what could happen to a blind chick on the road." During the trial, the girl went to the judge's house, told him the simple story of this kindness, and kept Keith out of the slammer. He was ordered to perform a free concert for the blind. Keith described the outcome: "It had to be one of the most bizarre sentences of all time: 'He was caught with an ounce of heroin and he got sentenced to do a concert for the blind.' That one's got to be in the annals of legal history somewhere, right?"

Through kindness comes love. Through kindness, mystical things happen.

It's the closest we can get to God. Through kindness comes absolution.

Keith calls the Toronto teen his blind angel. We all have those angels out there. Who knows—there could be blind angels hiding in the shoe department at Macy's or at a hot dog stand. They could come to your assistance when you least expect it. They may be blind, but they are rarely dumb, and you may need them when the long arm of the law reaches out and touches you in all the wrong places.

Be kind. It keeps you going.

And if you can, give anonymously. And forgive debts. (Two additional and not-so-widely-known but still very typical Keith maxims.)

14. APPRECIATE A NOMADIC LIFE—EVEN IF IT'S WITHIN THE CONFINES OF A SMALL TOWN.
"I like to see the ways the world's going round."

Move around. Change. See new things. Go where things are different, where there's different music. Follow where the arrows point, or where the dogs can't find you. Keep yourself open to transformation. There's a lot of world out there. The more you see, the more places you go, the more you are. And there's a bonus positive that comes from continuously moving: It keeps the cops at bay.

Observe your universe and the universes in your backyard.

As Descartes wrote, "Traveling is almost like talking with those of other centuries." Keep moving, keep seeing "the ways the world's going round"; all the while, though, keep one eye looking forward and one eye looking back (i.e., Commandment 15).

15. EMBRACE AND LIVE WITH BOTH THE PAST (THE GREATER HISTORY) AND THE FUTURE (POSSIBILITY).

Look at a photo of Keith's face. The left eye looks out optimistically, with youthful energy, to the future. The right eye is a bit sunken, introspective.

The left corner of the lip sags somewhat downward; the right side is slightly uplifted.

There is a balance between the optimistic future and an introspective look toward the past.

The face tells us a tale, leads us through history, and reveals secrets. And in Keith's face, it can be summed up as Here and There, at Once.

As Cicero wrote, "The face is the image of the soul." And you can see in Keith's face a certain philosophical viewpoint on time—a simultaneous view of the past, present, and future.

The necessity of being mindful of history is something we've been told over and again, as with the over-trod George Santayana quote:

"Those who cannot remember the past are condemned to repeat it."

It's also important not just to remember the past but to *feel* the past—as well as the present.

New Age philosophers stress the need to "be here now" and to feel the Power of Now. This is true and good, but being mindful of the full picture connects us with all of time—the present, the past, and the future that is to come—all of which is as much a reality as the moment we're living in.

As far as your own personal, possibly dubious past is concerned (which is, as Keith says, a ball and chain that follows you around), remember that you are entitled to "retire from military service" and put that past in *the past*. The past has legs and can follow you. But as with anything that's following you—an overzealous fan, the police, drug dealers who won't quit, Mick's groupies—you can put it in its place and look the other way. Sequester it in a back room at the Memory Hotel. Write a song about it, lock it in there, and throw away the key. Gone. Done. It might still be there, in a form of existence ... but you put it where you want it. Where it deserves to be. And where you have some control over it. The Memory Motel: You're the landlord and manager, in charge.

16. THE CREATIVE INHALE—BREATHE IN WHAT YOU LOVE.

"I snorted my father. He was cremated and I couldn't resist grinding him up with a little bit of blow. My dad wouldn't have cared. It went down pretty well, and I'm still alive."

Snorting your father's ashes. Wow. I wish I had thought that one up.

When the British magazine *New Music Express* asked Keith in 2007 what the strangest thing he'd ever snorted was, this comment about Dad was greeted with a storm of shock and horror.

Keith quickly recanted—said he was just joking.

Then he recanted again: Yes, it was true, he said, and he'd only pretended he'd made it up so as not to upset his dying mother.

Maybe he didn't want Mum to think he was planning to do the same to her.

It's true that a lot of what Keith has creatively inhaled over the years, beyond Dad, is within the category of "illegal substances" or "recreational pharmaceuticals," but he's also always exuberantly inhaled that which sustains him: music, family, friends, snooker, laughter.

According to Harold Schechter in a *New York Times* editorial, father snorting is not such a far-fetched notion. It comes from a custom of funerary cannibalism, which "springs from a profound and very human impulse: the desire to incorporate the essence of a loved one into your own body ... the belief that when someone close to us dies, the person lives on inside us—that he or she becomes an undying part of our own deepest selves."

Maybe we should all partake of this form of inhalation. And often.

Breathe in what you love.

17. BE TOUGH, BE BRAVE, AND DON'T GIVE IN TO THE DICTATES OF AUTHORITY.
"Ever since I left school, nobody has ever heard a 'Yes sir' from me. Apart from a few exceptions: in court and in jail."

It may not be as easy for all of us to get by with this assertion—but in our hearts, we can do it. The only dictate you need to listen to is that which comes from within.

If you're someone whose inner meter tells you that you're made to stay up late, stay up late. Defying authority is not a matter of spray-painting subway cars (although it helps). It's a matter of making yourself the real authority—as set forth in the first and second Keith rules of order—and not buckling to what others say should be. And within that, of course, know your limits. You can only go so far with certain types of defiance before they come back and get you. Don't get scared. As Keith says, "I don't get afraid. I get angry." There's more energy in anger. Just ask Johnny Rotten.

18. VALUE FAMILY AND FRIENDS, DESPITE THE NUTTINESS THEY CAN PROVIDE.
"The only way you can be like me is to have a good family."

On first glance, this would seem a shockingly un-Keith sentiment. The Outlaw? Waxing sentimental about family? But this is from the guy who was once the big-eared little tyke who went into a panicked state whenever he couldn't find his mummy in the pickup location after school was out. It's also the same guy who, when in prison, wrote one letter while staring up at the little square window of sky: "Dear Mum, Don't worry ..."

One wouldn't guess that Keith Richards is a mama's boy, but facts are facts. It ended up being a good thing. He treated his mother well. And after twenty years of estrangement from his father, they reconnected, became close friends and domino partners. Keith's father, former common-law wife, current wife, and children were all there at the concerts. His marriage is nearly thirty years running. He has never revealed anything intimate about his children's lives.

And while he's certainly not been the traditional father, or husband, or son, his family always knows where to find him and knows that his love is always there.

A word to the wise from Keith: Look out for your family, even if you have to do it in secret. It's always worked for him. You can bet it's part of the reason he's maintained a friendship with Mick Jagger since the 1940s. There are some good deeds being done on the sly. Even if you carry a knife in your pants, or have to wave a machete or a pistol at Ron Wood every now and again, it doesn't mean you're not loyal.

On family: *"If you get a chance at it, try it out, because it's one of the most special things that you'll get on the face of this earth. It gives you that final missing link of what life's about."*

On friends: *"The only way to find whether a guy's worth anything is to take a risk. Sometimes friends let you down, sometimes they don't. But you take the risk, otherwise you get nothing at all."*

19. SPEAK UP. HONESTY IS MEDICINAL.

Can you believe some of those things Keith says about Mick to the press?

And what about what Mick says about Keith?

And what Keith says about Ronnie? And what Ronnie says about Keith?

And what Charlie says about Mick?

Maybe not everyone can get away with it—but somehow for the Stones, it works. A bunch of bitches letting it all out. It's something to emulate.

It's better to get it out than to keep it in.

There's a rule here, though, with what you *let* and *don't let* out. Ever notice that for all the band members' going on about each other publicly, they don't give each other's secrets away? What they are letting out publicly is just a matter of opinion. It's petty stuff. Making fun of the evil twin's seriously embarrassing spandex jumpsuits, choosing to arrive onstage via the cringe-worthy choice of a cherry picker, or all that When-is-he-going-to-stop? Peter Pan prancing around. Or ripping on the girlfriends, who provide conversation as scintillating as talking to an open window. Or making fun of the evil twin's pretentions in politics. What is underneath is always kept quiet and honored. Notice that confidences are kept. Nobody's ratting anybody else out. Follow this rule. As it's often been said by those who know the man: "You don't break a promise to Keith." And you can be sure it works in the reverse. You can talk, you can vent, you can have a big mouth, but know the ethical limits, always. Walk over those lines and you're walking into "You fucked with Keith?" territory, and there's no darker woods than that.

20. TALISMANS HAVE POWER.

Going outside your front door can be like going into a battlefield, especially if you haven't called your parole officer. But you don't even have to pass the front door to be in the combat zone. We all need to feel protected—and protection can be found in simple bits and pieces. It can be something as elemental as a ring that reminds you of courage, or the scent of a perfume that calms you. A yellow rubber band with a message printed on it. A key hanging on a string hidden under your shirt. A tattoo that no one can see. How about a bit of metal and leather tied up in your hair?

Get a look at Keith: With all those trinkets and feathers in his hair, he's like a warrior adorned. There's strength to be found in all those things painted and pasted onto the body. It's an arsenal. There's power in what they remind us of or distract us from. They've existed through the centuries for a reason. Don't shy away from them. Get your own collection. Make use.

21. ACCEPT MAX MILLER INTO YOUR LIFE. (OR: IT'S ALL A FUCKING JOKE. LAUGH.)
"It's great to be here. It's great to be anywhere."—Max Miller

Before you accept the metaphorical concept of the Rolling Stones as a higher power and overlord, know that Max Miller is their prophet.

It may come as a surprise, but the prince of darkness has taken a good part of his philosophy, and some of his best one-liners, from Miller, a flamboyant British music hall performer of the 1920s through the 1950s. That line, "It's great to be here ... great to be anywhere," was a Miller staple, and it's how Keith routinely greets the audience.

Miller may not be as well-known today as he was back in his day, but he lives on in Keith Richards. Miller was known for taking his subject matter to dangerous, often untested limits—and that included his wardrobe. Miller's costumes were a mishmash of outlandish styles from various classes, cultures, and genders, slapped together in one slightly mad presentation. You could say the same about Keith's combination of polka-dotted bow tie, leopard-skin jacket, Moroccan scarf, pirate earring, Cuban boots, and women's jewelry. It's retro Max. Vaudeville and the music hall gone rock 'n' roll. As Keith said:

"Rock 'n' roll's greatest weapon is humor." All that's missing is a water-squirting flower on the lapel.

When the Stones were auditioning new guitarists in the 1960s and 1970s, if the auditioner didn't know a Max Miller routine, his application was trashed.

It is like giving a religious nod to the Marx Brothers. Humor will always save you. As Andrew Carnegie said, "There is little success where there is little laughter." Or from Victor Frankl, in *Man's Search for Meaning*: "The attempt to develop a sense of humor and to see things in a humorous light is some kind of a trick learned while mastering the art of living."

"Even ... when the cops are waking you up again, you somehow have to laugh."

Laughter is addictive. It's the best sort of addiction. Snort it in, and let it out. And tell a stupid joke or two every now and then.

22. EXPERIENCE IS "THE PRICE OF AN EDUCATION."

"Whatever happened—even if it was a drag—I learned lessons from it. And I got something from it ... I never worried about who took who from where. I figure it's the price of an education."

Pay the toll. And keep going. Don't look in the rearview mirror if you can help it. Press on the gas and motor forward. (Just don't crash the car again when taking off.)

The price of an education. It is a mantra to be repeated. It's money well spent. It may not always feel like it at the time, but trust the laws of fairyland economics. You'll get the money back at the other end of the trip as you come out of the tunnel. And probably in a larger amount, and with a tip.

"Keith Richards does everything once."

23. LIVE AND LET LIVE.

It's really a hell of a lot easier to go through life obeying this maxim. And it's also one of those lines that can look prettier in print than it is easy to put into action. After all, there are tons of morons and crapheads out there. But even the morons and the crapheads get to have their spot on the planet. It's all along the lines of *acceptance*. Just as you have essentially to accept yourself, you have to accept that those other people are out there too. Just like the Inner/Outer Mick. One easy way to put Commandment 23 into actual practice is first to master Commandment 21, i.e., Accepting Max Miller into Your Life. If you can find a joke in it, it's not nearly as bad. And if that doesn't work, remind yourself that it's just like when you see a pile of dogshit on the sidewalk. Nothing you can do about it. Might as well accept it. Live, and let the shit on the sidewalk live. Which brings us to the next tenet:

24. SHIT HAPPENS.

Mutter these two words, and it's like taking five milligrams of Valium. Acceptance calms you down. And like so many of the Keith Commandments, here's another one based on this notion.

Accept that shit happens. It's all a part of life. And if you think that shit is not going to happen, you might as well accept the fact right now that you're screwed. Shit does happen, and then it happens again, and then it happens a little more. So say the two words, out loud, under your breath, or silently, whenever something creepy goes down. It's like brushing away a fly. It's as easy as turning on a light switch or lighting the fiftieth Marlboro of the day. Click. Flick. Light. Shit happens.

25. WHEN YOU DESPAIR, REMEMBER: THERE'S ALWAYS THE FUTURE.

Things aren't always going to be as bad as they might seem at the moment. Sure, the moment might suck. So you fall out of a coconut tree. So you set a hotel room on fire. But time does move on, and there is—well, "always the future." The future will come … even when you're beset by the shakes during detox, or you see the men with the handcuffs coming your way once again. The laws of physics and science—time—is *still* on your side. Time does move on, time does heal, and these Beelzebub moments do come to an end.

If you can keep this in mind, you can get through it. If you see it as a bright shining star of possibility off on the horizon, a realm of "I'll get there," you have something to see you through the rough patches. It's a punctuation mark that Keith uses often when talking about something that was less than glorious, a fall into personal failure, a gig gone bad: "There's always the future." It's a ticket out of the present when the present doesn't live up to the hype of "be here now."

As much as they tell you that the present is a present, sometimes you feel you can do without the charity of the tainted gift. That's when the future really becomes your friend. And it can be a good friend.

26. PASS IT ON.

It's the same thing that Muddy Waters did. And Robert Johnson, and Buddy Holly, and Elvis. They passed on the tradition, the knowledge that came before—all that was experienced and learned. You learn it, you master it, you give it to the coming generations that follow you. And it's the message that Keith says he'd like on his tombstone: "He passed it on."

There are a lot of ways to pass it on and a lot of things to pass on—whether it be in lessons of kindness, or the playing of an instrument, or the understanding of all the blues (and other colors) in your life. Pass on love, kindness, good deeds on the sly, cheer, music, and wisdom. And through this act, you will continue on. Even if the process of acquiring the knowledge was more like passing a kidney stone, still, in the end, the art and the act of passing it on is one of the most profound actions toward immortality.

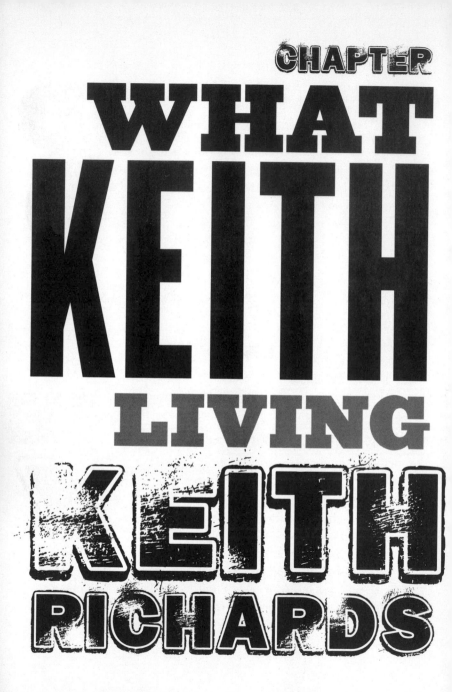

WHAT KEITH LIVING KEITH RICHARDS

SOLVING PROBLEMS BY CHANNELING YOUR INNER KEITH

The troubles keep coming: You fall off a
ladder in a library and are buried under the entire *Encyclopaedia Britannica*. You fall onstage in Frankfurt, slipping on a frank-furter. You fall onstage in Hamburg, slipping on a hamburger. You fall out of a tree. Your head is opened by surgeons for a look around. You innocently snort your father's ashes and are seen as a degenerate by the entire world when the news gets out. You're given six months to live. You live past those six months. You grimly go to the funeral of the doctor who gave you the bad news. You stay up for three straight days on purpose. Then you stay up for seven more by accident. You're banned from Japan. Your daughter is sent away to live with your mother because your lifestyle is too extreme. A teenager shoots himself in your house while you're away. Your girlfriend was reportedly in the bed where it happened (while she was also practicing witch-craft and playing Russian roulette). You fall asleep standing up and break your nose. You're given a permanent place on the international customs watch list. Every time you look around, you wonder if there are unmarked cars watching you. You're usually right. You're arrested at the airport when you thought they'd given up on that game already. Martin Scorsese watches it all from the sidelines without intervening. You're attacked onstage. You wake up with cops around your bed. You're spit on. Your hair is yanked. You're threatened with death. You're put on the most-likely-to-die list yet again. You're insulted by

being taken off the most-likely-to-die list and replaced by some amateur punk.

Maybe some of these things have happened to you.

Or maybe they will happen to you. There is, after all, as Keith says, always the future.

And when they do happen, if they happen, what do you do?

First: Accept the fact, as stated by Keith in Commandment 24, that "Hey, shit happens."

That's step number one.

That done, you have half the battle won.

Solving a problem involves 50 percent attitude and 50 percent technical know-how.

Fifty percent of each comes through the ability to channel your inner Keith.

Ask yourself: What would Keith do?

Never mind the other gurus and their instructional videos and manifestos. Never mind the people who expound on kindergarten lessons, or the one who whispers that she has a secret, or the guy with all those bowls of chicken soup. Here's a better path out of the woods.

A guy who has cheated death as often as Keith has, and come through it stronger than ever, has something to say about getting by with the allure and aesthetic of "The World's Most Elegantly Wasted Human"—an aesthetic that not too many gurus can claim, by the way.

What follows is an investigation into a series of fairly common problems (or their associates) and an inquiry into how to solve them—by asking and answering the question, *What would Keith do?*

Trouble comes in two basic forms: from the outside and from the inside. From other people, and from yourself.

Who do you have to run from? Who do you have to look at square-on? What do you have to learn to laugh at? How much do you have to silence that Mick? How much louder do you have to make that inner drummer? How much more do you have to listen to who you are? Which situation or person do you need to finally accept?

Trouble can be dealt with by way of the Twenty-six Ten Commandments. But there's another way to look at it, in Keith terms, that makes it less intimidating: Look at all the different types of trouble as if they're songs on an album.

You have the hit single, the one that you replay and replay and replay but still can't figure out the words to. You have the long, drawn-out number, which puts you to sleep and makes you nuts, and yet you still don't turn it off when it comes on. There's the song you can't get out of your head. You have the filler, which still somehow haunts you. And there's the big dramatic epic that is supposed to be the ending to it all but doesn't quite end, ever. But songs can be reworked, fixed.

They can be fine-tuned, played until they're right. In the end, what was a headache becomes a work of art.

But first you have to meet the headache, trouble, head-on.

And Keith will look it right in the eye. He'll then decide whether to continue the staring contest until trouble cowers in the corner, or whether he should hit the damn thing over the head with a guitar.

But by whichever means, he will defeat it. He's willed himself to. He's been through too much not to.

THE MANY SONGS
OF TROUBLE

Trouble with Other People:

I. STAYING STRONG: SELF-PRESERVATION AND JUST SAYING NO

"Just say no." Easier said than done. Too many of us have a hard time on this one. Saying no to people. Or places. Or things.

And then there are those little troll-like nags who come around with the whiny voice and *insist*. We keep caving, keep saying yes, and kick ourselves afterward.

The troll-like nags are getting you to do any number of things: drive them across town, do their Xeroxing, coerce you into buying stuff you have no need for or impersonating a dead spouse down at the public, assistance office.

How can we be strong enough to say no?

--- | **WHAT WOULD KEITH DO?** | ---

The down-and-out experience of drug addiction and dealing with the dealers may have lasted a bit longer than Keith would have liked, but he did get some lessons in etiquette out of it, as well as some ideas on inverse salesmanship.

Keith claims he learned how to be a gentleman from drug dealers. And his children say that they learned their manners from his postdrug gentlemanliness.

He also learned how and what not to be by watching how they *were*. It's like learning how not to make a bad movie from watching a bad movie: how not to be a jerk from observing a jerk.

The bad stuff teaches you the don't-do-its of life.

One other thing a drug dealer can teach you: the head rush that can be attained by saying no.

If only Nancy Reagan had had a summit with Keith—she would have been so much more effective.

When giving up drugs, Keith took the experience of dealers trying to sell to him and turned it inside out: "I just watched their faces when they couldn't make a sale—and that would be my high."

Give it a test run at a department store. You'll be surprised how effective it is.

How to do it? First, channel your inner Keith. Then look at the subject slowly and straight-on. Move slowly, keep up the stare, and say little. While one of the most potent weapons in life may be music, so is its twin: silence. Don't get rattled. No long, extravagant excuses are necessary. As Thomas Jefferson said, "Nothing gives one person so much advantage over another as to remain always cool and unruffled under all circumstances."

II. NOT LETTING THE TURKEYS GET YOU DOWN AND KEEPING YOUR HEAD ABOUT YOU EVEN WHEN ALL OTHERS ARE LOSING THEIRS AND BLAMING YOUR ASS FOR EVERY DAMN THING

Even if you've done your part in working within the construct that is the band, and you've kept in mind and worked with the higher power that is the Rolling Stones, there are still going to be slipups. Why? Other people.

Things just, well ... go wrong. It's just another damn law of nature.

Groups inevitably start falling apart. And what happens? Someone inevitably becomes the scapegoat. It's okay when it's someone else. But what do you do when the scapegoat is you? In a way, you can congratulate yourself: You've achieved Keith status. As Keith has said about himself time and again, "Whatever side I take, I know well that I will be blamed."

Take your pick of the subject: the declining morals of society. Pot-smoking teenagers. Nice girls turned tarts. Accidents on highways. Parties gone out of control. Capsized boats.

Keith's fault, Keith's fault, Keith's fault.

Getting blamed can be a compliment—it means you've got some influence. You've got to have some power in you to be awarded blame. In ancient Greece, people blamed the gods.

Scapegoating can happen in any number of situations.

You're blamed on the job and you're let go. You're running for public office, something goes wrong, and *boom*, you're the bad guy and out five thousand votes. Your marriage falls apart, you go before the judge, and his robed finger points at you as the gavel goes down. The dog dies: "It's your fault." The company goes bankrupt: "Why did you do this to us?"

Compliment or annoyance or downright soul crusher, you still have to know that blame is just a reflection of the finger that is pointing. And if they're going to blame you, rather than ruffling up in defense, make it work for you. See the experience as something to learn from.

WHAT WOULD KEITH DO?

"Who do you want to lay it on? Do you want to blame somebody, or do you want to learn from it? Altamont, it could only happen to the Stones, man. Let's face it—it wouldn't happen to the Bee Gees."

Ask yourself what you can take away from the experience. And then move on.

Don't look back in the rearview mirror. As one of the Twenty-six Ten Commandments said, experience is the price of an education. Just make sure that you check the receipt and that you don't buy the same thing again.

And if you feel you really need to give out some blame, use the Keith approach: choose someone who's not "here" anymore.

A Keith example: When longtime Stones crew member Chuck Magee died of a heart attack, the tragedy happened with typical Keith bad luck—during a concert. Keith turned around after a number and noticed Chuck wasn't there anymore.

But Keith turned the catastrophe around: "We've kept him alive—we blame him for everything that goes wrong."

If you've got to blame someone, find a phantom and blame the phantom. It's easier on everyone. The phantom might even enjoy it.

III. BETRAYAL AND TRUST

We'd all like to believe those wonderful, sugary sentiments—that all people are basically good, that what you put out is what you get back, and that kindness is in the hearts of all, ready to be retrieved with a gold-plated fish hook.

If only.

It's a nice thought to have in your head, but when you find out it's not always the case, it feels as if you've been thrown off a cliff, or off the balcony of a hotel.

There are all sorts of levels of losing your trust—like finding out that the guy you lent twenty dollars to in "good faith" had no intention of coming back with it the next day. Then there's the bigger stuff. Betrayal. The emotions it evokes can take on biblical proportions. For example: When you've entrusted someone with the intimate details of your life, and suddenly you find out they've spilled your secrets, what do you do?

WHAT WOULD KEITH DO?

Let's just go into the darkness on this one.

Jesus had Judas.

Keith had "Spanish Tony" Sanchez.

Imagine having a trusted drug dealer for years, and then he ups and leaves, goes away for a little while, and reemerges with a long, tell-all book complete with photographs and footnotes.

Say the word *Judas* and everyone knows what you're talking about. The guy spawned a million imitators. The Judas experience is unfortunately far too common. You don't see the knife coming. And when the stab comes, it's like a cold shower coming out of nowhere. Turning the other cheek is not necessarily the best choice.

And the Judases of the world need to know this. It shouldn't be so easy to get away with. Turning the other cheek is the last thing to do. Why get hit twice? Why fuck up your skin? Why give a Judas that option?

In this case, luckily, you have the cosmic universe working on your side as an assistant. Judases rarely win. It's just part of the laws of nature. Part of the cosmic order. It might take some time, but they always trip in the end. It's just a matter of time. And as anyone who has gone cold turkey once or twice can tell you: Time is the greatest healer. The Judas experience included.

First, once you pull the knife out of your back and wipe off the blood, accept that the secret is out. Nothing you can do to reel it back in. But the option you *do* have is what you're going to do with Judas, or to Judas. The obvious choice of a sock in the jaw isn't necessary. It's not worth the health of your fingers.

When Keith met up with Sanchez after the book *Up and Down with the Rolling Stones* was published, Keith didn't punch him out. Instead he showed him a new gun he'd bought. "I haven't seen him since." It wasn't a threat. It was the use of the Keithism "There's always the future." Keith showed him a ghost in a felt-lined case. Translated: Someone will come and get you, Tony, at some point. There's always the future. You just don't know where or when. It's the reason why that first Judas couldn't stop running, and went mad.

You don't need to go as far as Keith did and pull out the weapons. It's just a matter of letting them know, or more important, letting yourself know, that the future is always there, *that the seasons change*, and that eventually the numbers do even out. Just knowing this will act as a sedative. And if your Judas has a ghostwriter, that's even better. When Keith ran into Spanish Tony's ghostwriter, John Blake, at a wedding, and approached him about "that book," he got to see the image of a fleeing, running-for-the-wilderness Judas. Getting to watch a Judas flee from a wedding, pushing the bride out of the way, tripping over the cake, is worth the cost of the experience.

Don't be afraid of your Judas. Don't be afraid of those who are cruel and vindictive. As Keith has said about dealing with the demon: "If you confront him, then he's out of a job."

IV. WHY NOT ME?
Or: Being Passed Over For Honors That Go To Others

It feels good when you believe in yourself and tell yourself you will get what you deserve—that good things will come if you wait.

But sometimes it doesn't quite work out that way. Or at least not when you want it to. It's that little problem of watching good things go to others and not to you. Translated: You're passed over.

It can happen in any number of situations and scenarios: at home, in relationships, in love, at work.

Let's examine it close-up in the scenario of work:

You've been passed over for a promotion. It was given to the idiot one cubicle over. When something like this happens, your initial reaction may be to burn down the cubicle dividers or the drapery in the boss's office, or to pick the locks on the file cabinets, xerox the personnel files, and distribute them anonymously during the night. But are these instincts correct?

WHAT WOULD KEITH DO?

Okay: First off, put the basic kernel of the Commandments to work:
Accept it.

Things aren't always fair ... but you can make them more fair than they know.

Let's look at this problem at the office in further close-up.

Work, like Mick, is a necessary evil. We've heard that there are people out there who love their jobs, but who these people are is one of the great mysteries in life, like the workings on an open G chord. Work can provide an inordinately high supply of stress. One of its biggest headaches: Other People. Co-workers.

In learning to live life like Keith Richards, the best way to deal with a difficult or distracting co-worker is to view him or her as the Mick. Once defined as that necessary "other half"—the one, according to the principles of Keith, that exists in order for us to exist, and whose reality must be tolerated—this person suddenly doesn't seem quite as daunting anymore. With attitude and vision adjusted, we can manage the problem more easily.

Within this specific work scenario, comparison can be found in the horror Keith felt in being passed over for a knighthood when it went to Mick instead. It's bad enough that one should be overlooked, but being overlooked for your evil twin is all the more painful.

So what would Keith do? What *did* Keith do? First: Talk to as many people as you can. Speak specifically to those who will be able to transmit the most bad words regarding your adversary to the largest number of listeners. Let it out. Let it bleed. You're pissed. Say it. Eventually all the negative attention will focus onto the unworthy one, and this focus will bring up another question to those watching from the sidelines. Specifically: Was he worthy? Why *him*? And why did he even take the job? After all the complaining he did about the company, shouldn't he have passed it up? And now what? Will he mess up?

By inspiring so much negative focus on the unworthy one who took your knighthood—I mean chair—away, eventually you will cause him to trip, and you'll be there to take over. If nothing else, it will stir up and inspire much sympathy for you—and that's even better. Like time, sympathy is something that can be bent.

Moral indignation can be a good thing—as long as you get cast as the particular moral indignation's hero. Everyone loves to sign up for that fan club. So keep talking. There's no greater satisfaction than the one felt in getting royalty dethroned.

V. CHANGE, LOSS, AND WHEN YOU'RE TOLD TO GO

Fired. Broken up with. Divorced from. Evicted. Kicked out. No longer welcome.

They are all basically the same thing, just in different guises. When it comes, it's like having your left lung ripped out. You're pissed. It's painful. It disorients you. What do you do?

WHAT WOULD KEITH DO?

First, realize that you're not so special. You're more a part of the norm now that you've been banished. To give it a Keith term, it's exile. Maybe it's a heavy term, but it feels heavy when it happens, so you'd might as well pump it up with an equally heavy name.

In Keith's life, there's a significant chapter on exile. It even went on to become the name of the band's (maybe) best album. Keith went through a long period of exile in the 1970s. But, like a drug habit, he kicked it. And if Keith can do it, you can do it—you can take a disturbing condition and turn it around into something that sparkles.

Keith and exile started up their love-hate affair in 1969. He'd been flying high for years, in more ways then one. Suddenly, the rug was pulled out from under him. Not just one rug. A whole warehouse full of rugs. Realities were shifting. Fame became an affliction rather than a charm.

He was being cheated by the band's manager. There was the death of Brian Jones. There was the free concert at Altamont, which, instead of being the mini–United Nations model of harmonious living that Jagger had preached it would be, gave rock 'n' roll its very own miniature fallen Rome—a model of chaotic violence.

All good things must end, including the utopian 1960s, and when that happens, who are you going to blame? Keith and his fellow Stones seemed a good choice.

The government turned the screws. Their taxes were hiked; they were surveyed, busted. The queen was pointing toward the door. They packed their suitcases and moved to France. Cut off from home and roots, the band retreated into a dark mansion on the Riviera, which, in a double kick to the head, turned out to be a former Gestapo hideaway.

But back to your problem: You're exiled. What do you do? What did Keith do? There's really only one choice. *Screw 'em*. And tell yourself: *I'll show them*.

But you have to actually act on this conviction.

A method to get there: "Change the backdrop." It's a standard Keithism. Every time there's trouble, he moves and sets up a new background mural. He put it to use in 1967 after a major arrest by going to Morocco, and again, after prison, by going to Rome. He did it after the 1977 arrest. He did it in the early 1970s with France.

Get a new background. Move. It doesn't have to be anything as exotic as the Riviera. You can choose Pittsburgh if you like. Change not just the larger visuals but the little things you surround yourself with as well. Look for new images, new sounds. And from there, develop your own new images and sounds. In the Stones' case, it was the album *Exile on Main Street*. In your case, it can be your *New Shopping List*. Or a new relationship. A new look. A new candy bar you never tried before, now eaten every day. A new five-line poem that you wrote.

As Keith says, "We carry our past around like a ball and chain," but we're free at any time "to retire from military service" and start anew.

There's a lot of world out there. Exile leads to transformation. And from transformation we can reinvent ourselves and become free. And if you're really lucky, you'll get a hit record out of it.

VI. SEPARATION, REUNITING, FORGIVENESS, CONTINUING ON

Family. Friends. They come into our lives, they wander about, they leave, they come back. We see them, we don't see them. Sometimes things end without a clear reason.

What happens when you haven't seen a certain person for a long time, then there are some bad feelings, and you feel nervous about meeting up with them again?

WHAT WOULD KEITH DO?

For all the bad-boy imagery, Keith is known for maintaining long-term relationships, as well as for being gracious to those whom he meets for the first time and those who reemerge from the past. For Keith, so much from the past needs to be sequestered as water under the bridge. You have to look beyond a lot to keep moving forward, because in the end that's what's important: moving forward. The past happened. The past will always be there. The future we can do a little bit more with.

We've all done things we're sorry about. And while everyone knows that You Don't Cross Keith Richards, a typically Keith quality is also to forgive the past's misdeeds and keep going.

As long as they are within certain limits.

Just don't bilk him out of several billion dollars or call him an arthritic monkey. (Are you listening, Andrew Loog Oldham and Elton John?)

One Keith example of putting the past behind came by way of Marshall Chess.

After serving as the head of Rolling Stones Records, Chess found himself distanced from the band for eighteen years by "misunderstanding" and, well, "circumstances." When he finally turned up at a Stones concert years later, he was nervous about the reunion. He asked for five minutes to set things straight. Keith's response: "What the fuck are you talking about, Marshall? You were there. And now you're here."

Another example of this philosophy involved more complicated past histories: Nellcote, Keith's house in the Riviera, was formerly a Nazi headquarters. When a recording engineer was freaked out by the sight of swastikas in the house, and its potential bad spirit and dark past, Keith's response was, "But it's all right. We're here now. Fuck those people."

The Keith moral: The present moment, ultimately, is what has the most power. Embrace the present moment. Don't be afraid of what has happened in the past. Keep an eye on the future, but be here now.

VII. CONFIDENCE: HOLDING UP AGAINST CRITICISM
Or, In Keith Lingo: the Dean Martin Dilemma

Criticism is a bitch. Sometimes it is meted out on a level that goes beyond what seems appropriate and is nearly vicious. Then we question whether or not the person dishing it out is right. It makes you want to give it all up, pack up the bag. When you get it, what do you do?

———————————— | **WHAT WOULD KEITH DO?** | ————————————

When criticism is unleashed on you like a wild dog, you're sure the critic is getting an erotic thrill out of it. And maybe that's the case. Everyone needs to get their kicks somewhere, sadists included.

Keith and the Stones have taken on some choice commentary over the years. Some typical early 1960s reviews: "It is disgraceful that long-haired louts such as these should be allowed to appear on television." "The whole lot of you should be given a good bath ... Your filthy appearance is likely to corrupt teenagers all over the country." "I have seen today the most disgusting sight I can remember in all my years as a television fan."

Lovely.

But one of the roughest came in 1964, when the Stones appeared on the TV show *Hollywood Palace*. They felt they'd finally made it and were in the big leagues. But the show's host, Dean Martin, had other plans. Dino rolled his eyes and insulted the band in a continuous rant, often without the band realizing it: "The Rolling Stones. Aren't they great? [roll of the eyes; mocking laughter from audience] ... I don't know what they're singing about, but here they are ... Now don't go away. You wouldn't leave me with the Rolling Stones, would you? ... That [trampoline artist] is the father of the Rolling Stones. He's been trying to kill himself ever since."

Dino, how could you?

What do you do? Go back to the dressing room and kill yourself? Instead of losing hope, Keith got mad. What could have kicked in his confidence and sent him crawling home maimed instead only made him stronger. What doesn't kill you does make you stronger, like Nietzsche said—if you let it.

"If Dino had thought a little more, he wouldn't have been quite so flippant, but then I don't blame him thinking about it now. At the time it was like a deadly insult, but all those things only went to make us want to prove ourselves more, so that we could come back and bite their heads off. That was all they did, was like, steel you. That's what toughens you up."

It's just like the exile issue. Every time you hear a no, know that the no's true purpose is to be proven wrong. Half the time the person giving the no is on the way out anyhow. Not many years later, Dean became a relic. Seasons always change. As Keith says, *"There's always the future,"* and the future was honing in on Dean's turf. Time is a scary thing—but work with it. *"What is life but playing with time?"*

The higher purpose of these nasty comments is to remind yourself to keep tough and stick to your ideas. And it's here where the expression *An opinion is like an asshole, everyone has one* becomes meaningful.

The best part is when you can prove you were right, no matter how long it takes. Decades later, when accepting a Grammy Lifetime Achievement Award on behalf of the Stones, Mick spoke for all of them: "To all the people who took the piss—the joke's on you." It was a great moment of your evil twin coming through and telling it like it is.

However, even within your own Rolling Stones, there's going to be some fighting for your ideas. During the making of Stones records, when the band decides which songs to keep on an album and which to discard, Keith raises his hand for every song. "Eventually, they'll find their way."

Trouble Within:

VIII. BEING YOUR OWN SAINT GEORGE AND HOLDING TOUGH AGAINST THOSE "INNER DEMONS"

There's enough problems with the outside world and problems coming from other people, so isn't it a drag that there has to be so much turmoil and trouble on the inside as well? Most of it we never signed up for. It was just given to us as a gag gift from God. Everyone's got something: obsessions, addictions, neuroses. Things push and pull inside us. We've got to come to terms with them. But where do you start? Is there a poetically Keith way to handle it?

WHAT WOULD KEITH DO?

Inner demons.

Where do you look for the answer on this one?

Here, some help can be found by looking back to the cautionary tale named Brian Jones.

Jones, the founding member of the Stones who died at age twenty-seven from "misadventure," having drowned under mysterious circumstances in a swimming pool, had, according to Keith, a few too many demons—more than should be the daily requirement—which ultimately undid him.

Brian's demons ganged up on him, got him in the pool, wrestled him down, and won. It was just a matter of time before they won, and everyone knew it. Brian's demons fed off each other, multiplied and divided, ultimately took over, and destroyed him. As Keith has said: "Brian was effectively already dead when he died."

We all have an inner Jones. There's the inner and outer Mick, which acts as an organic yin-yang balancing act. And there's Charlie, the drummer within, who keeps you on beat and strong. And the Ron Wood—the gregarious sidekick to your larger self, who illuminates your good points. There's the Bill Wyman, the circumspect appendage that you somehow need but that might fall off at any time. And then there's Brian, the part of yourself that is more trouble than needed, that will eventually be sacrificed to make the rest of you work. Think of Brian as your appendix.

Brian is symbolic on many levels, from the petty to the sublime: from the dangers of being blond in the Stones to the danger of being slain by your inner demons. Brian did not take time to know himself. Or his limits. And in the end it killed him.

"There is a demon in me, but I only own up to having one of them. Brian probably had forty-five more ... He was so self-important, maybe because he was so short ... The thing with Brian was that as soon as he identified one, another would crop up. I've got just the one demon but he's bad enough ... My policy is to identify one and deal with that."

That is the Keith solution: Get it down to one. Also, try not to be short.

It might take some work—some mentally turning your demons into clay, then squashing them together into one lumpy demon—but you'll be better able to eliminate them that way. Think of it as crumpling up paper, or compressing a mass in a trash compactor, down to a small, puny size.

Once you're on the asphalt with the demon, "It's a matter of looking him in the face." And don't be afraid. Remember this Keithism: "The devil doesn't bother me, it's God that pisses me off. Him and his rain." The devil is an amateur.

IX. FRUSTRATION, ANGER
And: How Do You Release It?

Those inner demons are one thing. But then there's that other crap that slags around within. We can feel it with a person or a situation. Or with things going on out in the world, in the higher realms that are those metaphorical Rolling Stones. Sometimes it's with something as pathetic as an object. A pencil can easily do the trick on the wrong day. When frustration and anger come calling, what do you do?

WHAT WOULD KEITH DO?

This:

1972: Keith and saxophonist Bobby Keys hurl a misbehaving television out the window of a hotel balcony and exult in the moment as it's demolished several stories down, smashing like a box of lo mein on impact with the concrete. (They were good boys about it, though: very careful that no one was standing below, and that it was aimed at the garbage bins.)

Frustration has to go somewhere. If, according to the teachers of spirituality, material objects are secondary to living things, then, dammit, make *them* the outlet for anger and frustration, rather than living things. Choose from any of the following: TVs. Toasters. Chairs. Boxes of Cap'n Crunch cereal.

Another thing you might try is physical release via music. In living life the Keith Richards way, physical release and music are killing two mean birds with one stone. Music, when played by Keith, is music physicalized. You can see it in the way that Keith moves: The music is pumping through his arms, his legs, his neck. Emotion is made into something tangible.

However, if you can't take it to this physical extreme, you can make the fumigation/release through the elemental base of it all: art. Music, writing, visuals, or anything on the spectrum, pot holders included. It's one of the most therapeutic means of fumigation. For all his talk about good genes, I think that it's *this* that's kept Keith alive for so long: "There were times we felt like killing people, but we got out our guitars and wrote songs instead."

There is release to be found in the pen, in the human voice, in the lick of a guitar. And remember, with frustration, things like Mick can be a blessing in disguise—an adversary who can work for you. As Edmund Burke wrote, "Our antagonist is our helper," and,

"Never despair, but if you do, work on in despair." Frustration and anger can be good for you.

Keith's frustration and anger toward Mick came to the rescue many times during periods of creative stagnation.

"I'd written about forty songs for this album and I just dried up. Steven [Jordan] turned around, looked at me, and said: 'When in doubt, write about Mick!' ... In ten minutes, I'd written the whole thing."

You know the line: "Keep your friends close, but keep your enemies closer." This isn't necessary in physical form, but when it comes to art, don't push them too far away. Enemies make for the best art.

"If you stop singing about things that are distasteful, you're reduced to singing about embroidery."

X. HOLDING TOUGH WHEN THINGS GET ROUGH

We can feel as if we're spending our entire lives running from trouble. Just ask Keith. The only time he's not running from trouble is after it's already caught him.

For most of us, even though we think we don't have to hide, or that we're on the safe side of town, inevitably, it's going to show up. You might not see it coming. Or it might chase you down. You might outsmart it. But all too often, in the end, it's gonna catch you. It catches everyone. No one gets out of here unscathed.

But when it comes and clamps down its claws, what do you do?

| WHAT WOULD KEITH DO? |

Trouble. This is a subject Keith knows something about. It follows him around like a dog. They're on a first-name basis. They wear each other's perfumes.

Like Houdini, Keith somehow keeps getting away. And over time, he's picked up a few tricks to keep it at bay.

First, when he feels it's in the neighborhood, he puts up a Beware of Dog sign, and, via the Commandments, he *keeps moving*. Still, you're probably going to run into it while running—at a stop sign, or when you crash the car yet again. And so, as Keith says, "For the unexpected, you must be prepared."

What to do? Have a room ready, along with sheets and towels.

When trouble shows up and moves in, bring in a third room-mate: Max Miller.

Keith's life has often been reminiscent of a scene from a W. C. Fields movie—where Fields falls a hundred feet off a cliff, lands half on his feet and half on his ass, and then says in a slow, slightly amused drawl: "What a catastrophe." A similar Fields response came from Keith, right after his drug bust, when he was asked how he felt about the drama and anxiety of the experience:

"It's all just showbiz. My whole life is showbiz."

And was he worried about prison?

"I was wondering if the uniforms would have stripes or arrows."

Another way to deal with trouble is to ask yourself a question that Keith has asked himself in moments of trouble: What would Errol Flynn do?

Flynn has appeared in Keith's life many times. A longtime fan, Keith has lived at an old Flynn homestead, bought one of Flynn's old boats, and conjured Flynn's spirit. He's long been intrigued by Flynn's ability, whether on-camera or off- to elegantly jump away from trouble and keep moving.

So: What would Errol Flynn do?

Here's one answer: He'd learn to ski.

And that was what Keith did during a period when he was being heavily dogged by the junkie image and lifestyle. He moved to

Switzerland and taught himself how to sail down slopes. At first he was laughed at by four-year-olds, but with a little effort he became a master and was sailing past the tykes. If you're going to be a down-and-out junkie on the run, and people are whispering about you as a dark-eyed, ashen-skinned phantom of backstreet doom, why not throw yourself into a pursuit that is blaringly the opposite?

Skiing, at a minimum, is more fun than rehab.

XI. CREATIVITY

It's supposed to be the great solace. The thing that's uniquely your own, your heart and soul, blah blah blah. So why does it have to be so fucking difficult? You try to work on it, and nothing comes out. You're just sitting there, empty. You don't know how to begin. What do you do?

WHAT WOULD KEITH DO?

Some of Keith's greatest words of wisdom are those that focus on the creative process. Much of it revolves around the notion of the antenna. We all have one. It picks up the vibrations from the "universe" around us — even if this universe is our backyard. We need to *listen to the vibrations of the antenna*. Listen, and let what is being transmitted come through you. Let yourself be the vessel.

There are other techniques that can be put to use. While Keith is referring specifically to songwriting, it can be adapted to almost any of the arts.

1) Play it backward.
2) Take a break. Sometimes you have to go somewhere totally new, whether it's a new band or a new medium. In talking about getting out of the Stones for a while, Keith said, "You realized you were working for this juggernaut and you created it. This monster has taken you over. And maybe that was one of the things that made us take a crack at each other and work outside."
3) Play the works of others—from that, something new will come.

4) Replay pieces of your own, and from these works, you'll find that new gems are hiding inside, waiting to be coaxed out.

5) Don't despair. Remember that the best work is always ahead. When asked what the definitive Stones album was: "We haven't made it yet. It's definitely still to come." Don't ever give in to feelings that your best is behind you. "We keep going ... we never stop."

XII. HONESTY
It's not Always as Easy as all those Philosophers Lead You to Believe

Everyone's always talking about being "honest." Philosophers can't shut up about it. Keith included. But sometimes you have to wonder: Is it really necessary? Why do I have to divulge secrets? How much do I really "owe" people? When do I have a right to protect myself? And what is really so bad about telling lies—from white to slightly gray? What do you do?

WHAT WOULD KEITH DO?

One of the Keith Commandments is that nothing is a secret. You can ask him anything. Sometimes you might push it, and he'll make you feel like an acorn crushed flat under a heavy boot. But still, you can ask. It's part of the uniquely Keith charm and a defining characteristic: the ability to look squarely at all things and answer honestly. He's not hiding the past, what he's done, who he is. No hiding of the ravages behind Botox and plastic surgery: "It's all there, baby."

However, truth, like all things sacred and great, has its boundaries. It's the reason we have the word tact. The number-one Keith tenet is to be true to *yourself* and protect yourself. You don't need to give away all the truth all the time, and so freely, if you feel that there could be consequences.

"Bob Dylan was right—to live outside the law you must be honest," said Keith. However, if the press—or whoever takes on the metaphorical purpose of the press in your own life—is going to hound you, you can at least have some fun with it. If accusations are following you and upsetting you, you can always dress up the story like a Christmas tree. It they are talking about how you're a drug addict, *you* start the rumor that you go to Switzerland once a year for a full blood transfusion. That's what Keith did. You can always beat them at their own game.

When Keith was asked at a press conference if they always give the same answers to everyone, he said: "Hey. We've been at this twenty-five years. We dream up fifteen different answers for the same question."

The most important thing is that your stories not hurt anyone, and if you're going to tell a lie—don't lie to yourself. You're not likely to believe yourself anyway, and you're probably worse off if you do.

XIII. ENDURANCE
Or: The Chuck Berry Dilemma

You've just gotten a position with someone who is hugely regarded and admired. It's a big deal. But now you learn this person is beyond difficult. On the one hand, it's a great opportunity, yet on the other hand, you don't know if it's worth it, or if you will get through it. That seems to be the hardest part—to just get through it. What should you do?

WHAT WOULD KEITH DO?

In Keith lingo, it's the Chuck Berry Dilemma: "Chuck Berry ... He's the only guy who's hit me that I've never gotten back."

Imagine getting the chance to meet and work with your childhood hero—the person who literally got you into the profession you have chosen, and then you find out that the person is "the biggest cunt I ever met."

When given the chance to work with Berry in the making of the documentary film *Hail! Hail! Rock 'n' Roll!* and to perform at Berry's sixtieth-birthday concert, Keith took the job but made it something bigger than itself. It wasn't just the chance to play with his artistic idol. He turned it into a chance to prove himself to his band members, and he turned the experience into an exercise in strength and endurance.

It's just like a tennis match. You don't necessarily get into the game to win and take home the trophy—you play from beginning to end to see if you can *do* it, stick it through, and come out the other end alive. It becomes a personal accomplishment, a personal battle star: I played the game, sweated it out, felt tired, took a few hits, but I made it to the end. I survived the hardest tennis match, in the sun. I survived Chuck Berry.

But when getting into a situation like this, how do you prepare?

1) Before you even start, remember: Always know your limits. If your limits prove that it's something you can't do or take, don't. But if you decide you can, onward to number two.

2) Change your job title (if only to yourself). No matter what title they give you, cross it out in your own mind and replace it with what it really is. In this case, for Keith, he made it the S & M Director.

3) Humanize your opponent. "Even Michelangelo probably thought he was third-rate." This is where another Keith tenet will steel you: "We're all the same under the skin," childhood heroes included.

4) Then, give it the full Max Miller touch. In getting ready for the Chuck Berry gig, Keith said: "I ordered the straitjacket, and allowed six to eight weeks for delivery." He turned it into not only a test of proving he could do something, he made it a Max Miller routine.

5) Put a time limit on the experience.

If you can see it purely as an endurance test—engaging in a game, walking a marathon, or playing a difficult song to the end—what you come out with at the end is: *I did it*. And not much feels better than that.

As Keith says in *Hail! Hail! Rock 'n' Roll*, "If I can do this, I can do anything."

XIV. WINGING IT, FAKING IT, AND JUST DOING IT

What happens when you're getting into a situation that you're not at all prepared for? It's one of those "new and unknown" scenarios—a new living situation, a new town, a new school, a new relationship. It's all new to you, and you're nervous about how it's going to go. What do you do?

WHAT WOULD KEITH DO?

Remain optimistic and spontaneous, and "keep breathing." These are the roads to stay on. Added to this, make use of the brilliant tool known as the blues.

There's so much in the blues that is about spontaneity and improvisation, working off the moment and the other players. If you listen to those around you and wing it, you'll create more "beautiful accidents."

"It's not Bach or Beethoven. It's not like you've got to play it this way, note for note. You get out there, you know the feeling. The whole thing is about improvisation. Here comes the blues again, and it keeps coming ..."

With this, make use of the Keith concept of weaving, where you work two guitars together as one. With weaving, you don't try too hard to take control, and you work in a give-and-take with the other players.

So much of life is like going up on a stage, and with so many gigs, you just never know what's going to happen. Wing it. If you see winging it as being like the blues, it becomes an artful activity. Or, put in a more base way:

"When it's time to go on, it's time to go on, and when you get up there you either croak, puke, fall over, or not."

XV. ALWAYS KEEP GOING

Completely overwhelmed? Feel like you can't take another step forward? Want to give up? Not sure you can keep going? The end of the road?

WHAT WOULD KEITH DO?

"Keep breathing."

This was the answer Keith gave *Mojo* magazine in 2007 when he was asked what life's biggest lesson had been. A bit of a surprise for someone who could have spouted a long and complicated lesson about how to get away from sirens and prison bars, using gymnastics worthy of an episode of *The Monkees*. No. Just:

Keep breathing.

CHAPTER THREE

KEITH AND OR: THE OF KEITH AS VIEWED GREAT

NIETZSCHE
PHILOSOPHY
IN RELATION TO THE
PHILOSOPHERS

> "The point of philosophy is to start with something so simple as to seem not worth stating, and to end with something so paradoxical that no one will believe it."
>
> — *Bertrand Russell*

> "All are lunatics, but he who can analyze his delusion is called a philosopher."
>
> — *Ambrose Bierce*

Who would have guessed that a heroin-addled guitar player from the projects would end up as a twenty-first-century philosopher and urban street guru?

But this brings up the question: *What* exactly makes and creates a philosopher? Or a prophet? Or a guru?

There are two reigning camps on the philosopher scene: You've got the suave side and the disheveled side. There's the princely aristocratic thinker with the fancy-schmancy university degree and the walking cane. Then there's the other guy—the one who got into the palace through the back door by picking the lock. It's the prince and the pauper. Goofus and Gallant. Guess which one Keith is?

In the first camp are the guys whose lives are devoted to the quiet cloister of the ivory tower. The other kind walks through the fire, then emerges on the other side with blisters on his feet and fingers, the smoke still hissing out his ears ... and yet he's done it—he's become someone wiser and kinder and enlightened, someone who now connects and speaks to the *people*. Once out of the fire, there is now beauty and a message to be found in the blisters, scars, and smoke. It's here where we find the prophets of the Bible and the long lineup of saints, with their bad behavior spun as if by Rapunzel into a halo of gold. Oh, those prophets ... with their jaunts across the desert, their long stretches of lost sleep and heart-to-heart talks with burning bushes, their battles with demons in sandstorms, their secret conversations with God while eating stale crusts of bread delivered by pigeons, their hallucinations of strange music. And then onward to ducking when stones are flung, getting tossed into a cage or a prison, laughed at and poked with sticks, put before a court of judges. This is the road Keith Richards walks.

And yet there are some Keith connections to both sides of the philosopher aisle, both old school and prophet school. Throughout philosophy, all those who have illuminated the pressing human questions of "What do I do?" have also served another function: to illuminate the sayings of Keith Richards.

And then Keith illuminates them back.

☠

By looking at the wisdom of the great philosophers—both the Goofus and the Gallant schools—you come closer to the final goal: bonding with the Keith Way of Life, seeing it clearly, and achieving a full rendition of the Tao of Keith in daily living.

🔪

It's the Keithaholic's job to show how you can chart the entire history of Western philosophy by way of Keith Richards. You start with the Greeks, wind upward through the rationalists, take a right turn into the Enlightenment and empiricism, upward into the land of the humanists, make a left down into the brooding Germans, onward into the transcendentalists and downward into the valley of the existentialists, stop briefly at Mae West, and then continue on until you're footnoting Wittgenstein and the complexities of language.

And while Keith has something in line with all of these luminaries, there are a few philosophers who seem to have a more pointed connection to Keith—even if that connection doesn't, on first glance, present itself with glaring obviousness. But look a little closer and you'll see that they're speaking the same language.

☠

It starts, of course, with the Greeks: Socrates, Plato, and Aristotle. The three-sided think tank. Looking at the Greeks in everything–Keith Richards terms, they were the model of a perfectly working band: Plato on drums, Aristotle on guitar, and Socrates doing lead vocals. Working in tandem, they created something bigger than themselves.

Alfred North Whitehead wrote that all later philosophical writings—Keith's included—are but footnotes to what was laid out by the Greeks. There are certain subjects where Keith is specifically footnoting Plato, Socrates, and Aristotle: the mystical nature of music, the essence of friendship, and self-understanding.

"Knowing yourself" was first attributed to Plato and Socrates, as illustrated by the well-worn line, "The unexamined life is not worth living." By the time it gets to Keith, the maxim is illuminated by the man who has faced death more times than is deemed normal yet keeps going, knowing that *nobody* can tell him who he is and what he should or shouldn't be doing. He knows himself and his limits.

The Keith idea of "passing it on" was also set down by the Greeks. Socrates passed it on to Plato. Then Plato passed it on to Aristotle, then Aristotle wandered the globe and passed it on to Alexander the Great ... and onward and onward again, passing on riffs and knowledge. Aristotle even painted a picture of Socrates as "that wise old man" who dispensed advice and imparted down-to-earth, easy-to-understand moral teachings—just as Keith has noted about the wise bluesman.

Keith Illuminates the Greeks and the Greeks Illuminate Him Back

"The hardest victory is over self."—Aristotle

"For a man to conquer himself is the first and noblest of all victories."
—Plato

Keith: "I'm here today because I have taken the trouble to find out who I am."

"A true friend is one soul in two bodies ... a friend is a second self."—Aristotle
Keith: "Mick's rock. I'm roll."

"We are what we repeatedly do. Excellence, then, is not an act, but a habit."
—Aristotle

Keith: "I play the guitar a couple of hours a day, and something will come."

"There is no harm in repeating a good thing."—Plato

Keith: "Look at Jimmy Reed: For twenty-five years he did the same song, and every one of them is different."

And: "There's really only one song ... and Adam and Eve probably sung it ... and everything else is a variation on it."

"Music is a moral law. It gives soul to the universe, wings to the mind, flight to the imagination ... Music is the movement of sound to reach the soul for the education of its virtue."—Plato

Keith: "Music is a language that doesn't speak in particular words. It speaks in emotions, and if it's in the bones, it's in the bones."

"It is not wisdom that enabled [poets] to write their poetry, but a kind of instinct or inspiration such as you find in seers and prophets who delivered all their sublime messages without knowing in the least what they meant." — Socrates

> **Keith: "Songs are running around—they're all there, ready to grab. You play an instrument and pick it up."**

"The introduction of a new kind of music must be shunned as imperiling the whole state; since styles of music are never disturbed without affecting the most important political institutions." — Plato

> **Keith: "It was jeans and rock 'n' roll that took that wall down in the long run."**

"If a man neglects education, he walks lame to the end of his life." — Plato

> **Keith: "Nobody stops growing, otherwise there's no point in doing the trip in the first place ... You keep learning, and you never stop."**

"Bad men are full of repentance." — Aristotle

> **Keith: "I don't regret nothin'."**

Then there's Saint Augustine (A.D. 354–430). Which may come as a surprise.

Keith and Augustine didn't see eye to eye on everything, but on the matter of the eye itself, they did. Both had an interest in investigating the senses and how the senses can fool us. They both had a particular suspicion for visuals. In *The Confessions*, Augustine warned his readers to beware the lures of the senses and not give in. In Keithism, the message bends a bit: You can indulge, but be careful. To add a line from evil twin Mick: "It is okay to let yourself go, as long as you can get yourself back."

Both Keith and Augustine came to their philosopher posts by

surviving lives of "sin" and excess. For Augustine, it started with stealing pears — then graduating to excessive brothel visiting. He later chose to live pear-free and celibate, but his vivid memories and experience of sin made him an expert on the subject. Just like Keith.

Augustine assured his readers that one didn't have to worry about being "evil," since all experience was a part of God's plan. This acceptance of the darker side of human nature is also very Keith Richards.

Augustine converted from sinner to saint, giving up a "bad" life for a "good" one, and Keith too has, in a sense, been converted. While he has never quite given everything up, he has stepped away from one aspect of sin — he pulled himself out from spiraling into the abyss, from being sucked away for good. He's also given up guilt. You might as well give up guilt if you're going to sin anyway.

If you're going to sin, then sin elegantly.

Like Augustine. He gave sin some glamour. He made it into an exotic vacation destination, a past where the wild things lived. He spoke about it as a travel reporter, as one who got out of the jungle. Both men used their lives as sinners as lessons for the examination of personal struggle, and taking on that "wild animal called life."

Keith Illuminates Saint Augustine, and Saint Augustine Illuminates Keith

"I admit that I still find some enjoyment in the music of hymns ... I realize that when they are sung these sacred words stir my mind to greater religious

fervor and kindle in me a more ardent flame of piety ... I also know that there are particular modes in song and in the voice, corresponding to my various emotions ... able to stimulate them because of some mysterious relationship between the two."— Saint Augustine

Keith: "Every sound has an effect on the body ... you are fighting some primeval fear that you can't even rationalize."

"The senses are not content to take second place."— Saint Augustine

"I must confess how I am tempted through the eye."— Saint Augustine

Keith: "Why can't video find its own niche in life and get off music's back?"

"The eye is attracted by beautiful objects, by gold and silver and all such things."— Saint Augustine

Keith: "The eyes are the whores of the senses."

"Love and do what you will."— Saint Augustine

Keith: "This is who I am. I do what I do ... Don't try this at home."

"Lord give me chastity and continency. But not yet!"— Saint Augustine

Keith: "Good. More for me."

Leap ahead a few thousand years, and we find Keith footnoting the Enlightenment, and specifically John Locke (1632–1704), the guy who loved the line "All men are equal"— that is, the basic sentiment expressed on Keith's skull ring.

We all have a right to life and to liberty, the right to rebel against unjust rulers and laws. (See the Keith Commandment on Authority, aka Commandment 17.) For Locke, knowledge comes through experiences and our place within the physical world, with an emphasis on the importance of *life* right *now*, rather than the afterlife. A good life is one in which our minds are free from superstition and constraints. Or, as Keith said with less floweriness: "I never went in for superstition ... I never did kiss the Maharishi's feet."

Keith Illuminates John Locke and Locke Illuminates Keith

"The only fence against the world is a thorough knowledge of it."—Locke
Keith: "I've seen everything."

"To love truth for truth's sake is the principal part of human perfection in this world and the seed-plot of all other virtues."—Locke
Keith: "There's nothing *worth* lying about ... Lying ... is a very destructive way to live ... I have nothing to hide. I found that's the best way to get along with everybody."

"New opinions are always suspected, and usually opposed, without any other reason but because they are not already common."—Locke
Keith: "What have they got a hard-on against a rock 'n' roll band for? ... This shit could change the balance of the world. A five-string fucking guitar and a couple of guys are gonna change that? When all of this shit went down in Europe here the last few years, that's when I realized it. No wonder they were a little uptight, because they saw more of the potential than I did at the time."

"All men are liable to error and … under temptation to it."—*Locke*

Keith: "This music is all about beautiful fuck-ups and recoveries."

❦

Following behind Locke: Rousseau.

Like Keith, Jean-Jacques Rousseau (1712–1778) is seen as representative of the time in which he lived—yet he lived outside the norm. And like Keith, he argued for feeling over the strangleholds of too much reasoning, the need for speaking plainly and honestly—in Rousseau's case, "confessing"; with Keith, "telling it like it is"—no holds barred, taking the dark side and laying it out without hiding it behind a mask or a curtain.

Rousseau's notion that "Man is born free and everywhere he is in chains" mirrors Keith's concept that music—and rock 'n' roll in particular—gets to the root of a human in his natural state and the core of his being.

Thus: Rousseau equals Keith Richards. Sort of.

Keith Illuminates Rousseau and Rousseau Illuminates Keith

"The world of reality has its limits; the world of imagination is boundless."
                                                                    —*Rousseau*

Keith: "If you can write one song, you can write nine hundred. They're there."

"When something of an affliction happens to you, you either let it defeat you, or you defeat it."—Rousseau

Keith: "I've watched it from above, saying, 'I'm a goner. This is it. No way am I going to survive this.' And by some quirk of fate you're actually still alive when the whole thing is all over, and suddenly ... boom ... you're back in the driving seat again."

"Absolute silence leads to sadness. It is the image of death."—Rousseau
Keith: "Rock 'n' roll—it's like a heart machine."

"Every man has a right to risk his own life for the preservation of it."—Rousseau

☠

Keith and Søren Kierkegaard (1813–1855):

The two share an interest in investigating the sheer absurdity of the nature of being. Plus a shared interest in bringing the emotions of humans to a heightened state—in line with the emotionally charged honesty of songwriting—and looking at the dark side with compassion, that is, not writing about embroidery. Rather: Express the messier stuff (like "Gimme Shelter" or "Midnight Rambler"). Humans are limited and fallible, and only through recognizing this can we develop self-understanding and not sink into all-out despair. Individuality and self-acceptance are most important: Let the emotions bleed out.

Keith Illuminates Kierkegaard and Kierkegaard Illuminates Keith

"Be that self which one truly is."—Kierkegaard

"Face the facts of being what you are, for that is what changes what you are."
—Kierkegaard

Keith: "All I know is myself."

"Life can only be understood backwards; but it must be lived forwards."—Kierkegaard

"Life has its own hidden forces which you can only discover by living."—Kierkegaard

Keith: "You have a life. You live it."

"During the first period of a man's life the greatest danger is not to take the risk."—Kierkegaard

"God creates out of nothing. But he does what is still more wonderful: He makes saints out of sinners."—Kierkegaard

Keith: "Ever since I kicked it and cleaned up, I've been bombarded with requests and offers to make a statement about this, or address judges. I've been asked to do lectures for judges! The chance I've been waiting for—FUCK YOU!"

"It belongs to the imperfection of everything human that man can only attain his desire by passing through its opposite."—Kierkegaard

"Life is not a problem to be solved but a reality to be experienced."
—Kierkegaard

Keith: "I like the expanding vision of life, of what goes on. I find it a fascinating story ... a great book."

"The highest and most beautiful things in life are not to be heard about, nor read about, nor seen, but, if one will, are to be lived."—Kierkegaard

Keith: "I'm Keith Richards. I try everything once."

"Trouble is the common denominator of living. It is the great equalizer."—Kierkegaard

Keith: "Trouble ... I'm waiting for the next hit."

And finally: Keith and Friedrich Nietzsche (1844–1900).

Nietzsche, like Keith Richards, had a penchant for trouble and getting blamed. Nietzsche just took it up a step further. World War II, for example.

As with Keith's penchant for getting blamed for murders, drug busts, fires, fights, and the downfall of a polite society or two, getting blamed was a great Nietzschian talent. Maybe greater than Keith's. And it really wasn't Nietzsche's fault. (It was while he was temporarily indisposed with insanity that Nietzsche's sister reportedly went to work on his manuscript, editing it to fit the eventual interests of Hitler.)

But beyond this bond over blame and trouble, both Keith and Nietzsche have a few other similarities that make them centuries-divided twins. Both lived as nomads, and both had their own personal Anita Pallenberg (for Nietzsche, it was Lou Salome). And, like Keith, Nietzsche also wrote poetry and music (not that good, apparently), becoming "the musician's philosopher"—at first inspired by Wagner, and then in turn inspiring compositions by Schoenberg, Strauss, Stravinsky, and Mahler.

And both Keith and Nietzsche looked at life, for the most part, in the Keith Richards Way: examining the issues of art, music, and individuality, and questioning authority. For Nietzsche, a Keith ideal was his concept of "stoic heroism," in which we must be strong and confront the ugly and difficult things about ourselves without buckling—a call to look these self-realities square in the eye, accept them, and then just live life for its own sake. We should live to the utmost of our ability—as we would wish to live in eternity. The "eternal recurrence of time" will thus bring us nearer to eternal life. Therefore, "Dare to become what you are," and be free to choose the values you want. It is from this base of essential ideals that Nietzsche's often misunderstood concept of the Übermensch—or the superman—came about, which was essentially a blueprint for Keith Richards, if you ask me.

Keith fits the job description of the superman in more ways the one.

Needed: a creative, incredibly strong individual who rises above the norm, is able to hold steady to his ideas and values, and is able to create new art and meaning out of chaos; a superstrong creature whose strength seems beyond human. Perhaps someone who will be the only survivor, along with New York City cockroaches, after a nuclear holocaust ...

Nietzsche Illuminates Keith and Keith Illuminates Nietzsche

"In the end, one only experiences oneself."—Nietzsche

"He who has a why to live can bear almost any how."—Nietzsche
Keith: "I have to live with me ... And I would follow me anywhere."

"Is not life a hundred times too short for us to bore ourselves?"—Nietzsche
Keith: "Boredom? To me, that's an illness."

"Only sick music makes money today."—Nietzsche
Keith (on mediocre musicians): "Everyone's a load of crap. They're all trying to be somebody else."

"Life without music would be a mistake."—Nietzsche
Keith: "Music is a necessity. After food, air, water, and warmth, music is the next necessity of life."

And: "You can build a wall to stop people, but eventually, the music, it'll cross that wall."

"That which will kindle the lightning must for a long time be a cloud."—Nietzsche
Keith: "The blues … it's part of everybody … It can be dark down there, man."

"Distrust all in whom the impulse to punish is powerful."—Nietzsche
Keith: "In the business of crime there's two people involved, and that's the criminal and the cops. It's in both their interests to keep crime a business, otherwise they're both out of a job. So they're gonna look for it. They ain't gonna wait for it to happen."

"I teach you the superman. Man is something to be surpassed."—Nietzsche
Keith: "What would kill other people doesn't kill me."

"Be careful when you fight the monsters, lest you become one."—Nietzsche
Keith: "There's nothing wrong with the gun. It's the people who are on the trigger. Guns are an inanimate object. A heroin needle's an in-

animate object. It's what's done with it that's important."

"If you gaze for long into the abyss, the abyss gazes also into you."—*Nietzsche*
> Keith: "At our best, we master the art of going just over the edge of the abyss, then pulling back."

"You need chaos in your soul to give birth to a dancing star."—*Nietzsche*
> Keith: "My music ... is about chaos. It reflects my life, and probably everybody else's."

"What does not destroy me makes me stronger."—*Nietzsche*
> Keith: "I'm still here."

"The secret of reaping the greatest fruitfulness and the greatest enjoyment from life is to live dangerously!"—*Nietzsche*

"Two great European narcotics—alcohol and Christianity."—*Nietzsche*
> Keith: "My biggest addiction, more than heroin, is the stage and the audience. That buzz—it calls you every time."

☠

If the history of all of philosophy is a matter of footnoting and expanding the meaning of a thought by adding to it, there's something Keith in all the great philosophers.

A Sampling from Western Philosophy, Illuminated by Keith Richards, and an Assessment on How to Be a Guru by Looking at the Keith Experience:

"The no-mind not-thinks no-thoughts about no-things." —*Buddha*
> Keith: "Brains have probably screwed up enough things as it is, and rock 'n' roll is better left to instinct, you know."

"Music is the art of the prophets and the gift of God." —*Martin Luther*
> Keith: "All music is holy."

"All life is an experiment. The more experiments you make the better."
> —*Ralph Waldo Emerson*
> Keith: "I looked upon myself as a laboratory."

"In the end, it's not the years in your life that count. It's the life in your years."
> —*Abraham Lincoln*
> Keith: "You uncover fragments of the past every time you think back. It's like a broken mirror. And every now and again you get a glimpse of what happened."

"The world was my oyster, but I used the wrong fork."—*Oscar Wilde*

Keith: "Some people would say I've had it easy. I just made it hard for myself."

"Everything that irritates us about others can lead us to an understanding of ourselves."—*Carl Jung*

Keith: "The only things Mick and I disagree about is the band, the music, and what we do ... He's my best friend and my worst enemy."

"I thank God for my handicaps, for through them, I have found myself."
—*Helen Keller*

Keith: "It kept me in touch with the street, at the lowest level."

"Do not be inaccessible."—*Baltasar Gracian,* The Art of Worldly Wisdom

Keith: "I'm up for anything ... I'm fair game. ... Ask anything."

"Fame is like a river that beareth up things light and swollen, and drowns things weighty and solid."—*Francis Bacon*

Keith: "I fell into it. I'm still falling."

"Hell is other people."—*Jean-Paul Sartre*

Keith: "Chuck Berry ..."

"When choosing between two evils, I always like to try the one I've never tried before."—*Mae West*

Keith: "If I knew what the other original sin was, I would do it."

"Just remember, once you're over the hill you begin to pick up speed."—*Schopenhauer*

Keith: "It's like wine, man, they [blues musicians] just get better."

"The first forty years of life give us the text; the next thirty supply the commentary on it."— Schopenhauer

Keith: "Some things get better with age. Like me."

"Honesty is the first chapter of the book of wisdom."—Thomas Jefferson

Keith: "I've got nothing to hide."

"Death is not an event in life: We do not live to experience death ... Eternal life belongs to those who live in the present."—Wittgenstein

Keith: "Don't call my coffin."

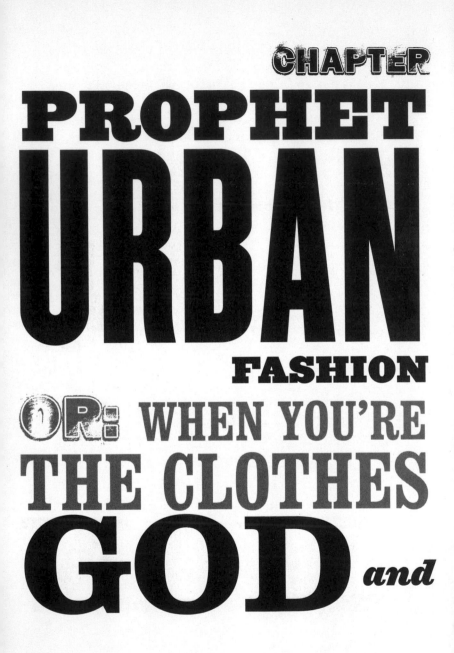

CHAPTER

PROPHET

URBAN

FASHION

OR: WHEN YOU'RE
THE CLOTHES
GOD *and*

FOUR

WEAR:
GURU

& STYLE
CONSUBSTANTIAL, MAKE THE
the MAN

"They are rare, those who imposed their style."

—Yves Saint Laurent

"Style is self-plagiarism."

—Alfred Hitchcock

"You don't find a style. A style finds you."

—Keith Richards

You may be thinking, "You've got to be kidding."

Or: "You're talking about fashion and style when it comes to the path of enlightenment and accepting a prophet into your life as a guide? How shallow can you be?"

Very shallow.

There are sharks and jellyfish swimming in the shallow end of the waters, not just in the deep end. You have to protect yourself and look for armor, answers, and help in all life's elements.

Anyone who views the human animal's outer shell of clothing and adornment as merely a frivolous layer of icing and vanity is kidding themselves. Fashion has always been a snarling, complicated language. Don't listen to the language, and the outcome can be deadly. If someone with a blue-streaked face, circa 25,000 B.C., went beyond the tribal boundaries and ended up in the yellow-streaked zone, it was all over. All fashion is boundary-laden, message-whispering, drenched in politics. Wear the color purple in the

Middle Ages when you're not a member of the church? You're toast. Wear bright red in the streets in 1770s Boston? Good luck. A neck choker in postrevolutionary France? You're in league with the guillotine's departed. Even the cowboy boot was an antagonistic reaction to the Civil War.

So when it comes to someone as culturally provocative and, let's face it, visually intense as Keith Richards, there's definitely more to the picture than just some Brit with a penchant for eyeliner, opting for a look a bit to the left of Young Republican.

For a man whose life has been so fraught with run-ins—the law, the press, sleazy managers, drugs, Chuck Berry—it is inevitable that the outer visual shell has some teeth. We all wear the scars of our battles.

And just as Keith maintains he's a vessel through which songs and lyrics are channeled, he's also an unwitting visual vessel for the historic (and personal) times within which his body has moved and breathed and snorted. It's the polyester-and-leather version of the "antenna." Images and experience come through him and are given back. And when he gets them back, they're often with polka dots and shark fangs.

Sometimes there's a residue of a doctor's diagnosis in what gets translated as "fashion." Kurt Cobain's grunge look came about partly because he was so consumed by insecurity that he hid behind ill-fitting clothes. Bob Dylan's dark sunglasses: not just about being groovy. He also had a vision problem. Issues of exhibitionism and insecurity get tallied in for Jim Morrison and Janis Joplin. And we don't have to get into the maybes regarding Michael Jackson.

With Keith, there's some trouble at the doctor's office that gets translated as well. There's the addict. There's the hounded, hunted man on the run. The guy who was given to shyness, who needed to wield a bicycle chain to get across town as a kid. The man who had a longstanding battle with authority and was given to bursts of violence, kicking the occasional asshole in the teeth when needed.

The personal battle created a visual armor—spiked hair, eyeliner, shark's-tooth earring, Middle Eastern soldier's scarf, leopard prints, hair tchotchkes, head schmatas, skull rings, handcuffs—all blended into a shell, a battlefield uniform to hold up against the world. As Machiavelli wrote, "Hence it comes about that all armed prophets have been victorious, and all unarmed prophets have been destroyed."

But Keith Richards wasn't always this image we've come to know. It took a while to get there, just as the process of being a guru does. In *The Bob Dylan Encyclopedia*, the metamorphosis of Keith is outlined thus: "Over time shifting from an amiable-looking mod with the street-cred cool of a bewildered rabbit, through the long heroin-happy years as Britain's licensed bad boy, to the extraordinary figure he cuts today as everybody's favorite cadaver. What's remarkable is how long his dark, hip makeover took him."

If only we could all remain an innocuous garden mammal. But things tend to change when the shit hits the fan. If you put a Barbie doll in a blender by mistake, when you take it out, if it's not completely shattered, it's going to look a little different.

The visual symbol that is Keith Richards—the one that is as recognizable as a box of Cheerios or a drawing of Charlie Brown—came about in installments, with each part pegged down after a period of significant trouble.

If fashion and style are an outcome of "something happened," then Keith as Cheerios box came about, in part, as a response to guilt, death, badgering, humiliation, and a little problem with policemen.

The Cheerios-level Keith got its first installment in 1967, the year some have called the period of the Great Keith Richards Makeover.

Keith was at a crossroads. One direction spelled defeat, the other spelled resistance, escape, and freedom. He decided he was going to get tough and take route B. Then he added the necessary armor and travelware. The journey, in prophet terms, was the first several miles of a walk through fire. And it was from this point on that a tougher Keith emerged. All accounts of Keith, post-makeover, attest to a guy who wasn't so shy anymore, who wasn't afraid to yell back, who started sharpening that now razor-fine wit. The prophet within started talking. Before that, he was just a rabbit in training. Then the rabbit went punk, and a philosopher was born.

Following the drug bust and the prison stint in 1967, the backdrops were briefly changed, first to Tangier, then Rome. It was in Tangier that he picked up the shemagh (the traditional Middle Eastern scarf used to shield soldiers from overexposure, sandstorms, and overbearing sun) that has morphed over the years into longer and longer versions with more and more skulls. It was also in 1967 that the hair got a little more dangerous, the protective darkness around the eyes more pronounced, and the sense of "Don't fuck with me" and "I don't give a fuck" grew more pervasive.

In Rome, Keith added a surprising new layer: woman's wear. When a guy wants to toughen up, you wouldn't assume that adding women's clothes and makeup would do it— but the woman he was taking it from was Anita Pallenberg, a gal who probably could have singlehandedly taken on half the NFL.

Keith also added on more bits from the Max Miller wardrobe: conflicting prints, polka dots, mad stripes. Near-vaudeville outfits. But if you're going to arm yourself against the beast, you might as well use humor. And if you have to dress like a music-hall comedian like Max Miller, or like Groucho Marx, or Laurel, or Hardy, or Buster Keaton, or Woody Allen, well, that's one way to survive.

Two years later, following the death of Brian Jones (who mistakenly did mess with Anita), Keith added the Peruvian shark's-tooth earring, another warding-off-the-demon talisman.

Jump ahead about ten years, and the war got uglier. The prophet in flames needed more protection. It was 1979, the next do-or-die period, and the most profound aspect of the Keith look came in: adornment on the finger and the wrist, a message about freedom, mortality, and equality forged in heavy metal.

First, there is the skull ring—given to him in '79 on his thirty-sixth birthday. During this time there were rifts with evil twin Mick and with Anita (capped off when a teenage boy shot himself while in bed with her). The band was unraveling. (Guess whose fault that was?) There were the aftershocks from ten years of junkiedom and nearly being done in by "getting caught." The ring gave him a sense of being grounded, its skull and bones acting as a continuous visual memo: Always be mindful of your mortality. Time and emotions are not to be wasted; the moment should be seized. *"Beneath the surface, we are all no more than bones."* Like Keith, we should repeat this to ourselves when the inner evil twin preens, or when we're feeling of lesser value than others. Keep the mortality of others in mind. No one is going to be around forever—no ruler or co-worker or asshole three seats down on the subway. It goes for the people who are giving you a hard time and for the people that you are giving a hard time.

The skull ring holds the same talismanic power of any religious symbol worn on a chain and used to ward off evil, keep one in line with God, or help a person remain devoted to an oath. And right alongside that skull, there's the handcuff bracelet, a reminder that prison is just a heartbeat away, that liberty and freedom can be lost in a moment and should never be taken for granted. And along with this, don't forget about life and freedom's evil twins, death and incarceration, who walk in their shadow.

And then, of course ... there's the Keith Richards hair ...

🔪

There are differing reports on the meaning of all that stuff in there (a Chinese coin, a Maltese cross, some beads, some feathers, some leather strings ... a few unidentifiable objects). Some say that his kids and friends just tie things up in there when he's passed out. Another explanation, which seems the most Keith, is that these trinkets are picked up on his travels, and that putting them on his head is a way of connecting to the world as a place greater than one's self, a metaphorical higher power like the Rolling Stones multiplied by a million that he can keep near him at all times. What lies on the body closest to the head or the heart is the closest to your inner being. Keith is not content with just having skin. He picks up pieces from the world and keeps them as a part of him.

It's the same with the scarves, which are sometimes gifts from fans or thrown onstage. He takes them in as tokens of the affection from the outside world and incorporates them into his everyday wardrobe. Items of flourish around the neck, feathers, and hair trinkets are also traditionally the talismans of the warrior— particularly the American Indian warrior—that give strength on the battlefield. You can see that in any picture of Sitting Bull (to whom, by the way, Keith has taken on a spooky similarity in some of the later photos).

Keith's hair has always been armor (spiked like a weapon, full of metal). It's also always taken on the purpose of a philosopher's wig. Look at the timeline of the great philosophers, and 80 percent of the time you're going to see big hair as an accessory of the great mind. Just look at the lineup: Spinoza, Leibniz, Descartes, Locke, Schopenhauer, Einstein. Big hair, big hair, big hair.

And Keith has added one other philosopher accessory to the big hair—the head shmata, originated by Plato (again, go to those history books—he's wearing it!), which was reprised in later years by David Hume, Jean-Jacques Rousseau, and George Berkeley.

Over the years, in true Keith fashion, many aspects of the armor didn't stay put within Keith alone. He extended it, blended it to work with his bandmates. Maybe they've left him alone with the head shmata and hair trinkets, but some of that outlaw armor has been spread out and shared, especially by his very own version of Mini-Me, or Keith Richards Jr., aka Ron Wood. Now, when you see the Stones coming in a pack—with long Max Miller coats, leathered faces, dark glasses, crow haircuts—it's like a posse of outlaws, and you'd better get out of the way.

Unless you want to join them.

All you need to add is the final defining characteristic, the swagger (just summon the image of a panther walking down the gritty sidewalk of a city), and you're in.

So what does all of this assessment of the Keith Richards style have to do with the path to enlightenment and learning to live the Keith Richards Way and accepting Keith Richards into your life as a way to save your ass?

Learn from the master.

If you're wandering around in hot pants and a crew cut and feel like something's missing, maybe there's a reason for it. Pay attention to the signals you're being sent—as to where you need protection by way of cloth and amulets.

And, most importantly, adorn yourself as only you can. If the number-one Keith tenet is to know yourself and to be true to that particular, unique being, go for whatever the signals are telling you to shellac onto that outer shell.

It's back to the notion of the purple hair of Commandment 1. If that's who you are—purple hair—do it. Take whatever you need to answer the calling of knowing yourself. If all we have is our skin and our bones and what's under that skin and bones, we might as well put on top of it that which is unique to its calling. And make use of Commandment 17 as well: Don't give in to the dictates of authority on this one.

That is: Tell *Ladies Home Journal* to go fuck itself.

CHAPTER FIVE

WISDOM OF

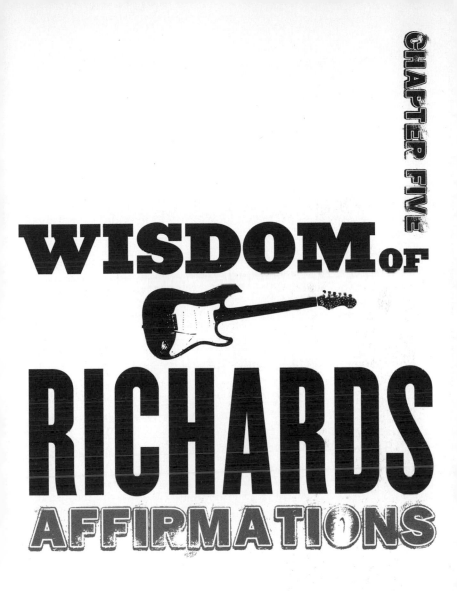

RICHARDS
AFFIRMATIONS

APHORISMS FOR LIVING LIFE THE KEITH RICHARDS WAY

THE AFTERLIFE and REINCARNATION

"The next world. What are we looking for? Promotion? Demotion? We're here living this life. What's the whole speculation about the next one? It'll either be there or it won't."

"I don't know about scuttling around on clouds playing cards."

"There's something out there ... But I can't tell you, I've been sworn to secrecy."

"I dunno what it's like singing with a dead man. I've never done it. Don't call my coffin."

> —on a "new" Beatles single, released after
> John Lennon and George Harrison's deaths

"I'll just take three slaves with me."

> —regarding the afterlife

"I never got a postcard from anybody that left. Maybe they don't sell stamps up there."

AGING and LONGEVITY

"Some things get better with age. Like me."

"Getting old is a fascinating thing. The older you get, the older you want to get."

"When I was younger, I said, 'If I live to thirty, I'll shoot myself.' You reach thirty and put the gun away."

"I like the expanding vision of life, of what goes on. I find it a fascinating story; it's like a great book. I'm two thirds of the way through it, and I mean, I can't wait for the ending, but I can put it off for a while."

"It's a fascinating process, just growing up. And it doesn't matter—anyone who's fifteen today, in thirty, forty years ... it's gonna take 'em a bit of luck to hit sixty-five. It's how you deal with that process."

"Unfortunately, our lives are sometimes bombarded with, you know, decay."

"We've all gotta age."

"It's a privilege. Then again, it's felt like a privilege just to wake up to a new day for a few years now."

"It seems strange that we do the same thing with the same boys all these years later. But it's like when you get drunk at a bar and wonder later how you got home. You know where you are—you're home—but how did you get there? That's the mystery."

"I never considered I was actually pushing it anywhere near the danger limit, although later on I realized that I was probably a lot closer than I ever admitted—but it kept my feet on the ground, nearly underground, in fact."

"I was Number 1 on the Who's Likely to Die list for ten years ... I was really disappointed when I fell off the list."

"Some doctor told me I had six months to live and I went to his funeral."

"As you get older, younger people think you know where it's at. But it's a forlorn hope. Because everybody's growing up at the same time, you know."

"The one thing I can't handle really well is that sudden change of pace in living. I can handle it through slowing down or speeding up; that's easy. But I just haven't got any brakes."

"Nobody ever wondered why the bluesmen were onstage until their old age ... It's the same with us. Why does a dog lick his balls? Because he can! We play because we can. We do what we have to."

"It's like we've gone over the equator. We're Magellan."
—*on the Rolling Stones' longevity*

"It's like one of those old maps where there are dragons, and it says END OF THE WORLD. Where is it? You don't know. You're supposed to fall off here."

"Do you know that I actually have a bus pass in England? I've reached the age where I am given a free bus pass. I feel like going to England right now and riding every bus I can get!"

"It's very nice to be forty years old in the band. I'm a lot older in real life."

"It's about a little bit of introspection and having a sort of physical contact with the mind and the brain. Having some connection ... I don't know what you'd call it ... religion? Or just call it lucky?"
—*answering the question as to how to stay alive*

"There's a certain thing about growing old, which I'm still getting used to. It's a whole new experience."

"Maybe age does matter, in that you consider time in a different way. You start to use it more, rather than clambering all over it and using it as a scaffold."
(SEE ALSO TIME)

"We're still learning and we never stop. You never know it all."

"The quest is: Let's find out how long a rock 'n' roll band can go. Nobody knows because the music's not been around for that long."

"We're the only band to make it this far, and if we trip and fall you'll know that's how far it can be taken."

"We all know somebody who we know is not going to be seventy, ever. Not everyone makes it."

"There were plenty of times I could've given up the ghost. But it just seemed such a cheap way out."

"Somebody has to find out how far you can take this thing, and I guess it might as well be me."

"Well, look at Duke Ellington. Or Louis Armstrong. Nobody argued about them going on and on."

"People should say, 'Isn't it amazing these guys can move like that? Here's hope for you all.' Just don't use my diet."

"The idea of retiring is like killing yourself. It's almost like hari-kari. I intend to live to a hundred and go down in history."

"The older you get, the more proud you are of getting there, because you know that half the suckers down the road, they ain't gonna make it."

"Why in the world would you stop doing what you like to do? If we ever do a tour and nobody turns up, then I go back to the top of the stairs where I started. I'll just play to myself."

"I will write all of your epitaphs."

"I wanna do it like Muddy Waters did it—till I drop."

"Maybe that's the answer. If you want to live a long life, join the Rolling Stones."

"I'm not Nostradamus, pal."

—*when asked how long he thinks he'll live*

"We're still going to be here when nobody's listening to your jokes."

BEING ALIVE

"It's great to be here. Hey, it's great to be anywhere."

—*often-repeated line when he greets a concert audience, taken from an old Max Miller routine*

"I would rather be a legend than a dead legend."

"As far as I'm concerned, life is all you get and I'll make the best out of it ... And so I decided to learn to live with myself."

"To me, life is a wild animal. You hope to deal with it when it leaps at you."

"Life."

—*when asked what his favorite journey is*

"Waking up."

—*when asked what he considers his greatest achievement*

"People think I know what I'm doing. Okay, I'll fool them! It's a bluff. The important thing is what comes next, and are you ready for it?"

"Living. Anybody else would be an idiot to say otherwise. You have a life. You live it."

—*when asked what the most important thing in life is*

AMBITION

"Unless you really want [something], don't jump in the pond. There's piranhas in there."

"A pool of piranhas. You want to get in there? You better not be tasty."

"Once you've decided that you want to be the best rock 'n' roller in the world, you go ahead and try it."

"You had to be the biggest dreamer in the world to think that you could export this stuff to America."

AMERICA

"If it works in America, then anything can happen."

"On our first expedition to the United States we noticed a distinct lack of crumpet."

"America was fairyland."

"Why the fuck is an American cop telling me to pour the national drink down the bog?"

—in response to a policeman in Omaha
telling him to dispense of the whiskey and
Coke in his dressing room, 1964

"America had all the things England had, only lots more ... It all seemed so exotic. The wildest countryside I ever saw was the marshes over the river Thames."

"America was where all our music came from, and there was the magical thought of going there with all the radio stations and being able to find all the records you wanted."

"To me, the biggest thing America had done this century—apart from throwing its weight around—was its music. A whole brand-new way, with so many different elements put together that never had a chance to be welded before. And it's still going on, of course."

ANGER (and CHANNELING IT)

"There were times we felt like killing people, but we got out our guitars and wrote songs instead."

ART

"As far as I'm concerned, art's just short for Arthur."

"I do not believe in having lessons. You only learn how some old geezer in their thirties wants you to play."

"If you just fancy yourself as being a big star, don't bother."

"I'm not into ratings. The day that I'm satisfied with what I do is the day that I give up."

"No other form of life on the surface of the planet needs art. That already makes us weird, as if it points a finger."

AUTHORITY

"The king is the man who can."

"If you're going to kick authority in the teeth, you might as well use two feet."

"After I left school, I never said 'Yes, sir' to anybody."

"Whatever side I take, I know well that I will be blamed."

"What really fascinated me was that they thought three Herberts with guitars were a threat to the social structure of the country."

—on the English government throwing
the Stones out of the country

"I love England very much. I think Buckingham Palace would be my preferred residence. But they kicked me out!"

"What's on trial is the same thing that's always been on trial. Dear old Them and Us. I find this all a bit weary. I've done my stint in the dock. Why don't they pick on the Sex Pistols?"

"When you think that kids, all they really want to do is learn, watch how it's done, and try to figure out why and leave it at that ... and they manage to turn the whole thing around and make you hate them."

"I thought it was ludicrous to take one of those gongs from the establishment ... I don't want to step out onstage with someone wearing a fucking coronet and sporting the old ermine."

—on Mick's knighthood

BAD EXPERIENCES

"I've seen murders. I've seen dogs come onstage trying to savage people. I've turned round and found a pool of blood where the piano player should be! I've been struck by sharpened pennies. But you can't really do anything about that. It's just a part of the gig."

"Yes, I've been trepanned. I've got pictures of it. They cut my head, brain, skull open, went in and pulled out the crap, and put some of it back in again. But that's the way it is. I mean, shit, Keith Richards has got to do everything once."

—on his brain surgery after falling out of a tree

"What goes down goes down, and it's how to deal with it that counts."

"Even being busted—it's no pleasure, but it certainly isn't boring. I think boring is the worst thing of all, you know, anything but boring. At least it keeps you active."

"I might get a song out of it."

*—on being asked at a press conference
following the Toronto trial what
the consequences would be*

BANDS

"The whole joy of making rock 'n' roll music is the interaction between guys playing."

"It must be obvious from the way the Beatles have split up and what's happened since. Although they're very good individually, now matter how much they say how little they worked together as a band, they did work together, 'cause nothing they'd done since has surpassed that."

"Most people don't know what a band is. The musicians are there to contribute to the band's sound. The band isn't there for showing off solos or egos. A lick on a record—it doesn't matter who played it. All that matters is how it fits. The chemistry to work together like that has to be there. It's not an intellectual thing you can think up and just put there. It has to be there. You have to find it."

"It's tribal. We can actually assault each other on a regular basis and nobody gets pissed off."

"Bands take a long time—especially this one—to mature."

"It's addictive. And addiction is something I should know something about."

"Coca-Cola know[s] what their ingredients are. We only know there is four guys ... very different people ... but the chemistry is there. The ingredients are right. So it works. That's the difference between Coca-Cola and the Rolling Stones."

"There's no way you can say that any one person is the band and the rest are just padding. It is such a subtle mixture of characters and personalities and how you deal with each other. And if it works right, you never think about it yourself, because ... if you analyze it, you'll blow it. So you don't really wanna know."

THE BLUES

"It's probably the most important thing that America has ever given to the world."

"To learn the blues, it takes a while, and you never stop. I learnt how to learn the blues, but I ain't stopped."

"That is the whole fascination with rock 'n' roll and the blues — the monotony of it, and the limitations of it, and how far you can take those limitations and still come up with something new. It's the restrictions and the form and the monotony that make it so interesting."

"If you don't know the blues ... there's no point in picking up the guitar and playing rock 'n' roll or any other form of popular music."

"This music got called the blues about a hundred years ago, but the music is about a feeling, and feelings didn't just start a hundred years ago. Feelings start in the person, and I think that's why the blues is universal, because it's part of everybody. Muddy is like a very comforting arm around the shoulder. You need that, you know? It can be dark down there, man."

"It's an amazing form of music that has a strength and vulnerability which seems to me to be translated throughout someone's life. At nine or ninety, it's utterly timeless."

"You have to go through a bit of life, I think, in order to play the blues for real ... You gotta be able to have a few stories to tell."

"The only blue I knew was the school blazer I'd just shed."
—on being nineteen years old and touring
with blues master Bo Diddley

CATASTROPHE

"Hey. Shit happens."

"Oh, it's all show business. Every day of my life is show business."

CHANGE

"Nothing is static in this life—and thank God."

"I like to let things change. I don't like to put things in a cage."

"It's *gotta* go up and down. Otherwise, you wouldn't know the difference. It would be just a bland, straight line, like lookin' at a heart machine. And when that straight line happens, baby, you're *dead*."

CHARLIE

As Stephen Davis wrote in *Old Gods Almost Dead*: "There's an old saying among those who have known the Stones. It's that Mick wants to be Keith, and they all want to be Charlie ... He's genuinely hip, he's got innate good taste, and understands restraint. Charlie kept his family together, and he never got off on the star trip ... When the job's over, he goes home and feeds his horses."

Plus, Charlie is the only one who's ever punched Mick out.

"Charlie Watts is my absolute favorite. He has all of the qualities that I like in people—great sense of humor, a lovely streak of eccentricity, a real talent, very modest. He's always hated being a pop star."

"Charlie is the most modest, the shyest man ... the idea of stardom horrifies him, but he's managed to live with it."

"It's Charlie Watts's band—without him we wouldn't have a group."

"Charlie's quite an enigma—the quiet conscience of the Stones. A great English eccentric. I mean, how can you describe a guy who buys a 1936 Alfa Romeo just to look at the dashboards? Can't drive—just sits there and looks at it. He's an original."

"If only Mozart had had a really good drummer ..."

CHEMISTRY

We all have our personal laboratories. Life is an experiment, and it's just a matter of getting the alchemical or chemical combination right. We're all unwitting alchemists. Sometimes, if we pay attention to the chemicals we're putting in the beakers, it turns out all right.

"Chemistry was one of those subjects in school that I was never good at ... but I think it's the *unknown* bit—the mysterious spark—that does it."

"Sure thing, man. I used to be a laboratory myself once."

—response to a fan asking him to
sign his chemistry book

"There's something to be said for a certain chemistry between people that makes for a certain kind of music."

"I believe magic is only a combination of natural forces."

"Magic is a word for something that is power that we don't fully understand and can enable things to happen. I mean, nobody really understands about the effect that certain rhythms have on people, but our bodies beat. We're only alive because the heartbeat keeps going all the time. And also certain sounds can kill."

"My personal laboratory."

—on his body

CHILDREN

"They do more for you than you do for them."

"You think about a lot of things when you have a kid ... It's all full of purity and innocence, and it's just smilin' at you, and wants to kiss you and hug you ... feel you and touch you, and you never felt so loved in your life."

"It's that bit of love you gave your own parents, the bit you don't remember—your kid gives that back to you."

"It's like a missin' piece in a jigsaw puzzle. If you can keep that, instead of showin' them off—'Hey, I made this'—they made *you*."

"They keep reminding you of things you can't remember."

"I've never had to explain anything to them. It's not like, 'Oh, Dad, you're an outlaw.' What would Jesse James have told his kids if he had the time?"

"Even for a hardened old cynic like me, it was a fantastic thing seeing a baby being born. I'm a softhearted guy when it comes to kids and things like that. I just love it."

"My kids are the least of my problems; it's the grown-ups that screw me."

"Children are far too intractable for you to impose yourself on them. There's no point in having fights, because they beat you every time. Especially girls."

"Children are like songs to me. You don't bring them up. They kind of show you what they need, and you provide it."

"They give you that little bit—that important bit of living when you absolutely don't know shit about nothing."

CLICHÉS

"I love clichés. They're so true and so boring."

CONFESSIONS and ACCUSATIONS

"You can't accuse me of anything I haven't already confessed to."

CONFUSION

"Confusion is not the ally of peace and love."

COURAGE

"At least I faced it. It's the only thing I'm proud about in all of that period—that I faced up to it and said, okay, that's it, and it's all over ... I was looking down the bad end of the gun."

—on his Toronto arrest

CREATIVITY (see also WRITING and INVENTION)

"I'm just a vessel."

"Is it a distraction or is it a vision or God knows what? It's all different things."

"Everybody starts by imitating their heroes."

"There's really only one song in the whole world, and probably Adam and Eve hummed it to each other, and everything else is a variation on it in one form or another, you know?"

"Musicians and performers start off with a focal point of somebody before they discover themselves."

"First off you just copy, then eventually you start to find out if you can add your own thing to it. Rock 'n' roll in particular is based very much upon that ... they have somebody in mind that turns them on to do it in the first place. It's the old thing of, 'The real thing that you can do and leave behind is the thing that you pass on to the next lot.'"

"Like anything else, the more practice you have at something, the more you find room to maneuver and find out what your limits are and how to overcome them."

"Songs are a funny thing; sometimes I think they write you."

"People reach creative peaks at different times, and you never know when it's going to come again."

"A painter's got a canvas. The writer's got reams of empty paper. A musician has silence."

"I never *know* what it is I'm looking for, exactly, but when I hit upon it, I know it."

"I'm just working, chipping away at it, more like a sculptor. 'No, his nose isn't that big'—whack ... You keep patching it up until it feels natural. Nobody *creates* these things: You've just got to be awake with your finger in the air like an antenna."

"You keep searching for things you haven't heard ... I don't go, 'I created this!' ... I feel that you receive songs. I never sit down and say, 'Right, now I'm going to write a song.' I just sit around and play either piano or guitar ... Buddy Holly ... Hoagy Carmichael ... But usually after twenty minutes or so the fingers are moving somewhere else and you go, 'Incoming!' "

"You make a mistake or you *think* you made a mistake, but ... research that accident! ... I'll buff 'em up a bit and put 'em into recognizable shape, then transmit them, and that's basically how I feel about writing songs."

"You think if I knew I would tell anybody? The fact is I don't know. All I know is that they fly in right through the room, they go through concrete, they go through the air. I think everybody now knows that my attitude to songs is that I'm an antenna. I wait, I sit down and play an instrument. The only bit I do is knock it into shape."

—in response to a question of
where his songs come from

"You are just a medium, you just develop a facility for recognizing and picking up things and you just have to be ready ... like being at a seance; they just plop out of the air. Whole songs just come to you, you don't write it ... I didn't do anything except to happen to have been awake when it arrived."

"Sometimes we write songs in installments—just get the melody and music and we'll cut the tracks and write the words later. That way the actual tracks have matured just like wine—you just leave it in the cellar for a bit, and it comes out a little better a few years later."

"Look at Jimmy Reed: For twenty-five years he did the same song, and every one of them is different."

"As a musician ... what you do is fuck around with silence."

"That's one of the things about music; it's a hand-me-down ... Whether you sell a million records or never made one, if someone's heard you and you've turned them on to it, you'd done your fuckin' job."

"Hollywood is the end of the line for so many people. It's a killer, and if you're weak you can be sure it'll get you."

"This is not something you retire from. It's your life writing songs and playing is like breathing—you don't stop."

"There's nothing like the human touch."

"My job was the fairy dust."

"A lot of what Mick and I do is fixing and touching up, writing songs in bits, assembling it on the spot."

"In order to do what I do—turn people on—the band needs to be turned on first."

"I'm an unpure purist."

"I like people that know what direction they want to go in as opposed to what people might like. I can't stand people trying to second-guess the public."

"What goes into a musician's ear usually comes out one way or another."

"As soon as you stop retouching, or recording on the grounds that, like, ninety percent of the people ain't gonna know the difference anyway, you're really lost."

"You don't want to analyze it too much, because in the process you can lose it."

"If you want to do good stuff, you're aware that you can't play it safe—you've got to keep pushing the limits. Of course, that can spill over into your life."

"If I choose one, I'll be killing all my other babies."

—when asked to name his favorite song

DEATH and BEYOND

"I've had a few brushes with old death, he's kind of a friend of mine, actually, and if you hang around me you'll have a brush with it too."

"I snorted my father. He was cremated and I couldn't resist grinding him up with a little bit of blow. My dad wouldn't have cared. It went down pretty well, and I'm still alive."

"It was a life wish. It's knowing yourself. If I ever felt that I was really going over the top, I would've done something about it. I was just testing my limits. And I stayed, as far as I'm concerned, well within them."

—when told he had a death
wish for most of his life

"Up until the middle sixties, the most obvious method of rock 'n' roll death was chartered planes."

"I was number one on the death list for half of the seventies ... A lot of people lost money on me."

"I let other people do that. They're experts, apparently. Hey, I've been there—the white light at the end of the tunnel—three or four times. But when it doesn't happen, and you're back in—that's a shock."

—in response to the question, "Do you contemplate your own death?"

"I've been closer to death a few more times than a lot of people. And what I've found out is that whatever it is, it's worth waiting for."

"People's perceptions change radically when you croak."

"When I'm gone, I'm gone. Everybody else can decide what to do with me."

"Later."

—when asked how he would like to die

DECISIONS

"It was one of those moments where you have to make a decision: take it on the ribs or take a shot in the temple on the desk. All part of life's rich pageant."

—regarding his fall in his library, where he was suddenly attacked by, and buried under, the Encyclopaedia Brittanica

DESIRE

"No, but if someone can come up with something, I'll have it."

*—when asked if there's anything
he wants that he hasn't got*

THE DEVIL

"It's just a matter of looking him in the face. He's there all the time. I've had very close contact with Lucifer—I've met him several times."

"You might as well accept the fact that evil is there and deal with it any way you can. 'Sympathy for the Devil' is a song that says, 'Don't forget him. If you confront him, then he's out of a job.'"

DRUGS and ADDICTION

"I've never had a problem with drugs, only with policemen."

"I've never turned blue in someone else's bathroom. I consider that the height of bad manners."

"I gave up drugs when the doctor told me I had six months to live."

"If you are going to get wasted, then get wasted elegantly."

"I don't think there's anything fantastic been written under the influence of drugs that couldn't have been written without."

"You ain't gonna inject talent into yourself."

—on heroin

"When I was a junkie I used to be able to play tennis with Mick, go to the toilet for a quick fix, and still beat him."

"I come from very tough stuff, and things that would kill other people don't kill me. To me the only criteria in life are knowing yourself and your capabilities, and the idea that anybody should take on what I do or did as a form of recreations or emulation is horrific."

"The wife's always asking, 'Why are you lighting up another cigarette?' I tell her it's because the last one wasn't long enough."

"I *am* my drinking partner."

—*when asked if he misses having a drinking partner*

"Intoxication? I'm polytoxic."

"People think that it's a matter of recreation, and it ain't ... As I said before, the drugs to me was something, like, to get the job done."

"That period of moral ambivalence."

—*referring to his super-heavy drug years*

"Nobody gets up and says, 'I'm taking drugs and you should too.' It's only when they come busting into your room and then splash it all over the newspapers that anybody knows about it."

"Musicians don't start off thinking, 'We're rich and famous; let's get high.' It's a matter of making the next gig. Like the bomber pilots— if you've got to bomb Dresden tomorrow, you get, like, four or five bennies to make the trip and keep yourself together."

"All the people that I've known that had died from so-called drug overdoses have all been people that've had some fairly serious physical weakness somewhere."

"Showtime in the seventies was whenever I got up. It had nothing to do with what the ticket said."

"I wouldn't have written 'Coming Down Again' without that. I'm this millionaire rock star, but I'm in the gutter with these other sniveling people. It kept me in touch with the street, at the lowest level."

"Smack. It's a real leveler. I'm a superstar, but when I want the stuff, baby, I'm down on the ground with the rest of them. But at the same time, I can't say I regret going there."

"On one hand, they say the Rolling Stones and rock musicians in general are corrupting the kids, but if they just left us alone and didn't come looking for drugs, then nobody would know if we had a drug problem or not."

"I don't regret zooming into the dope thing for so long. It was an experiment that went on too long, but in a way that kept my feet on the street when I could have just become some brat-ass, rich rock 'n' roll superstar bullshit and done myself in another way. I said, 'No, I want to put my foot in a deep puddle, because I don't want to hang out up there in that stratosphere with the Maharishi and Mick and Paul McCartney.' It was almost a deliberate attempt out of it. I almost forced myself into that in order to counterbalance this superstar shit that was going on around us. It was almost a deliberate sort of attempt to get out of it. Like letting the broken tooth hang for five years—deliberate anti!"

"Music and drugs—I don't really correlate one thing with the other. One is what you're putting out and the other is what you're putting in."

"It's really difficult to kick it. But it ain't impossible. It's not like getting your leg blown off."

"You can sit twenty people around this desk, give them each five whiskies, and see how differently it affects these people. Some will be under the table, two will be completely sober, and another might be slightly tipsy."

"Narcotics are passed from one generation of musicians to the next."

"I was sort of into De Quincey's opium eaters a century too late."

"For at least five years, undoubtedly, I was the weak link in the chain."

"The only reason methadone's such a big deal in America is because a lot of people are making millions on it."

"Look at the astronauts. They're completely chemically regulated from the minute they start that thing until they come down."

"Somebody going into the last stages of the colors of the rainbow ... That's really a drag."

"When a rock star dies, it's got a very romantic tinge to it, but actually it's very sordid."

"You know, during World War II the number of junkies in America dropped to almost zero because they just policed the fucking ports properly. Which means they can do it if they want to, if they really wanted to stop it. But you can make more money out of heroin than you can out of anything else."

"When I listen to what I did under the influence—ten years of work—I don't think it either enhanced or impaired me. It didn't have that much to do with it. Some guys think dope is great for their music. Bullshit! I took drugs because I wanted to hide."

"The only recurring dreams I can remember are all on cold turkey, and it was always that the dope was hidden behind the wallpaper. And in the morning, you'd wake up and see fingernail marks where you'd actually tried to do something about it."

"I never thought I was wasted, but I probably was."

"I don't encourage anybody to do what I do, you know? Why should you? More for me!"

"Nobody's got the right to judge over what I am putting into my body, apart from myself."

"I learned how to puke properly."

*— in response to a question about what
his greatest accomplishments are*

"I'm happy to be off it ... I have become a lush."

—on heroin

"I looked upon myself, in a sort of romantic and silly way, as like a laboratory."

"There are drug overtones in about 1 percent of the band's songs, and Mick wrote them, not me."

"I'm glad it stopped when it did because I've really enjoyed going the other way."

"... and miraculously, due to abstinence and prayer, my teeth grew back!"

EMPIRE

"You realize how paranoid they must be, that if they get rid of a guitar player or two, everything's gonna be cool in the empire. All they did was illustrate their fragility."

"It will just absorb it [new art] until it's part of the establishment. That's England's big trick. After all, didn't they do it to the Beatles? Slap a medal on them."

"They know what I would've said ... they knew I'd tell them where they could put it."

—on why the British government
didn't offer him a knighthood

"To me, the monarchy is not that important. I tell you, none of them is getting near me with a sword. I kneel for no one."

"That Adolf. What a piece of work ... I sort of took a personal dislike to him the minute he did my crib in. I thought it was personal."

—on Keith's assertion that a V-1 bomb
was dropped on his house—and right
into his crib—when he was a child while
out shopping with his mother

ENDURANCE AND ENNUI

"It is tiring having to meet people all the time and be nice to them."

—when asked if getting old makes him tired

EVIL

"Cheese is very wrong."

—claiming it's the one thing
he won't put in his body

"When we were just innocent kids out for a good time, they're saying, 'They're evil.' Oh, I'm evil, really? So that makes you start thinking about evil. What is evil? There are ... others who think we are Lucifer. Everybody's Lucifer."

EXCESS

"I love it."

"You kinda get the message after you've been to a few funerals."

EXERCISE and FOOD

"I never exercise. I would say that if you tried two and a half hours with the Stones three or four times a week with a guitar round your neck, that would do it for you. Just about."

"I'm onstage with that guitar ... I defy any gym to come up with a stronger regime than that."

"Why do you think there's this three square meals a day? This is about factories. You eat, you go to work, you get a break for lunch; when you're finished you get your dinner. But people should never eat like that. They should have little bits every two hours."

"HP Sauce is harder to kick than heroin."

EXPERIENCE and EDUCATION

"Things keep happening to me."

"Some of it, you really want to unlearn."

"Anything you throw yourself into, you better get yourself out of."

"I learned more in those six weeks than I would have learned from listening to a million records."

—on performing live onstage as the
opening act for the Everly Brothers
and Little Richard in early days

"I just sort of drift. I can drift into anything. I'm fair game."

"I've always just tried to avoid doing anything that would make me cringe. Anything I do, I like to be able to live with."

"Not at all. Now that you mention it, I wouldn't mind trying it sometime."

> *—when asked if he lives like a monk*

"Keith Richards does everything once."

"Well, it means basically—I've seen everything."

> *—when asked what he meant when*
> *he said "I've seen everything"*

"I've done the chandelier, and the revolving table with the melon. I've done it all, mate."

> *—referring to trying the Kama Sutra*
> *specifically, but he could mean anything*

"I was looking for Leonardo da Vinci's book on anatomy. I learned a lot about anatomy, but I didn't find the book."

> *—on falling off his ladder when*
> *reaching for a book*

"I'm still learning every day. I absolutely know nothing about music except what I find out tomorrow."

"Keep breathing."

> *—when asked what the biggest lesson*
> *is that life has taught him*

FAILURE

"I was once a choirboy. Westminster Abbey, soloist. Then my voice broke and suddenly it was, 'Sorry, son, we can't use you anymore.'"

"Ever since Westminster Abbey it's been all downhill."

"There's always the future."

FAME

"The legend part is easy. It's the living that's hard."

"I fell into it. I'm still falling."
—regarding fame and the Keith Richards myth

"You do, occasionally, just look at your feet and think, 'This is the same old shit every night.'"

"I was nineteen when it started to take off, right, and just a very ordinary guy. Chucked out of nightclubs, birds would poke their tongue out at me, that kind of scene. And then, suddenly, Adonis! And you know, that is so ridiculous, so totally insane."

"It went straight to his head. Suddenly he thought he was six foot four. In actual fact he was only five foot six."
—on fame and its effect on Brian Jones

"I've been invented by the media. I'm just a minstrel."

"We wouldn't be here if it wasn't for screaming teenage pubescent chicks."

"The fact is I am sixty years old, and twenty-year-old chicks are still throwing their pants at me. It's ridiculous really."

"We certainly didn't wanna be rock 'n' roll stars. That was just too tacky."

"I realized pretty quickly that in order to control my own music, fame had to go along with it. So we figured we might as well learn to be famous for a bit."

"I'm all for a quiet life, except I didn't get one."

"Fame isn't something where you just sort of go, 'Okay, I'll be famous!' and take the ticket. When it happens, you better grab it."

"Being famous is okay, but in the courtroom, it works against you."

"You try living out of a suitcase for twenty years."

"At least for a year I can walk around and say, 'Do you know who you're talking to?' "

—on accepting his man-of-the-year award

"If I'm a guitar hero, I never entered the competition—I forgot to fill in the application form."

"They come up to me in the street and say, 'How do we get to be really big and earn lots of money? What do you have to do to make a good group?' and I say, 'Well, look, why don't you try starving?' "

"You set yourself up in this game. You're supposed to worry when they're not there. You're up for grabs out there. I've been living with that for most of my life. I don't think it's enough to die for. I don't think you should run away. Hey, just stop."

—responding to Princess Diana's death

"You'd constantly be going through this thing of one minute ... fanatical acclaim, and the next minute you'd go a few hundred miles and it'd be, like, 'Scumbags!' You'd be nobody, the lowest, lower than the town bum—at least they *knew* him."

"In the end, being pop stars was handy."

"I get paid while I sleep."

FAMILY

"The only way you can be like me is to have a good family."

"If you get a chance at it, try it out, because it's one of the most special things that you'll get on the face of this earth. It gives you that final missing link of what life's about."

"I cry quite often. I look at a picture of my grandfather sometimes, listening to music that he loved."

"I think families are great as long as they can get along. And if you can do it with a couchful, why not a worldful? How wonderful life would be."

"Sometimes the only thing you've got to hang on to is family."

FASHION and STYLE

"I reckon our style came direct from the Three Stooges."

"Hair's a fascinating thing. Ask Delilah."

"The sexiest thing a woman could wear? Being stark fucking naked."

"Fashion thinks more about me than I think about it."

"I just wore what I wore and people noticed."

"Once you get into fashion in music it has already diminished."

"I love books ... a well-dressed mind!"

"Everybody associates long hair with dirtiness ... Maybe it's a Victorian thing."

"I mean, a few chicks have had a snip here and there when I'm asleep. Those damned Delilahs! Otherwise ... I just walk into the bathroom and there's a pair of scissors ... I don't like people around me with sharp objects. That's my job."

—on haircuts

"A lot of what I'd learnt at art school came home to roost. About selling a look, an attitude, an image—like what kind of hair you wanted."

"We had a set of uniforms, but everyone kept losing his suit, so we decided to call it a day and go on as we liked."

"Look at this. I've got chains growing out of my hair. Should I see a doctor?"

—on his hair charms

"I wear ... whatever is available in my bag that's not in the laundry. And then I steal a few things."

—when asked who decides
what he wears onstage

"If I don't have this down my belt, I kinda feel undressed."

—referring to a six-inch bone-
handled knife in his waistband

FEAR

"Fear? As a kid, I knew it real well. I'm this little squirt, and every day when I go home from school, no matter which route I take, I'm gonna get beat up. It was around then that I banished it—fear. I learned how to take a beating and how to get a good one in now and again. It taught me to toughen myself up."

"The stage is an amazing thing. You're up there with the lights on you. From that position, as long as you can control and hold it, you can contain events. But the minute you buckle, it's over."

"I don't get scared. I get mad."

"I haven't really been scared since I was at school, stood against a wall with the school bully in front me saying, 'I'm gonna trash you,' and I'm saying, 'Go ahead, what can I do about it?' That's when I used to get scared. But when [the police] were on me ... I got scared for the rest of the country."

"To me, the truth is the more you give, the stronger you are. The more of a man you are. Who are you scared of? What's so scary that you've got to lock yourself up?"

"I'm terrified of dentists."

FEELING IT

"I don't think onstage. I feel. Once you get up there, you're who you are. A little bit of peace and quiet. Nobody is calculating. We're just feeling."

FREE SPEECH

"Freedom of speech is something that everyone is supposed to believe in but seldom does. Look what happened to John [Lennon] when he made that remark about religion! Up to that time we had been the subjects for the controversial quotes. Our manager decided to ban all interviews for a while and let someone else put their foot in it—someone did!"

FREEDOM

"I would have loved to have been a pirate. I am fascinated with the idea of standing on one's own two feet. The idea of freedom, of being responsible to oneself only, of accepting no authority. That's probably one reason why I became a musician. Because ever since I left school, nobody has ever heard a 'Yes sir' from me. Apart from a few exceptions: in court and in jail."

"Like Dylan says, 'To live outside the law, you must be honest.' "

"Nobody's ever totally free, and free from what? I think a lot of people don't even know what's holding them captive. Sometimes it's themselves."

"You try saying 'Guilty' twenty-five times. I could get very spiritual here, but I'll never forget walking out for lunch that day."

—on a defining experience in court

FRIENDSHIP

"I'll say, 'Charlie, should I go to Mick's room and hang him?' And he'll say no. His opinion counts."

" 'I'll kill you now, but your wife wouldn't like cleaning up all the blood.' "

—Ronnie Wood quoting Keith
during one of their quarrels

"The only way to find whether a guy's worth anything is to take a risk. Sometimes friends let you down, sometimes they don't. But you take the risk, otherwise you get nothing at all."

"It's a true friendship when you can bash somebody over the head and not be told, 'You're not my friend anymore.' That's a true friendship."

"I don't agree with that saying, 'You can count your real friends on one hand.' If that's so, then you ain't farming the right acres, because friends are everywhere."

"If you can count more friends than you've got fingers, then you're really lucky. Luckily, I can start on my toes. I don't know if Mick can fill a hand."

"You go up, you go down, sometimes you disagree ... But what do brothers do? Brothers always fight off and on ... In some ways, it keeps changing and evolving, in other ways, it's the same as when we're in the playground when we were four or five years old."

"Mick and I know what it's like to go hard knocks with each other. It's a tough and bitter battle, a war of attrition. But you can do that with good friends."

THE FUTURE

"You've got to be looking forward to something."

"I feel very hopeful about the future. I find it all very enjoyable with a few peak surprises thrown in."

GOD

"The devil doesn't bother me, it's God that pisses me off. Him and his rain. You wait until I meet the motherfucker. Doesn't he know who we are? We're the Rolling Stones!"

"You never know what the sound's gonna be like in those stadiums. You're relying on God, who joins the band every night in one form or another."

"I've got to do something about this guy God joining the band again."

*—regarding the unwarranted bad
weather at a California concert*

"The only thing about the in-his-own image thing is, who'd want to look like this?"

ON BEING GOOD and BAD

"The good die young ... but hey, where does that leave me?"

"It's funny, when you've done it all. I'm such a good boy these days."

"If I knew what the other original sin was, I would do it."

"After a show the wise man will take it easy, digest his food, then put himself to bed. But then there might be a knock on the door. And then, would the wise man really want to forgo a good party?"

GUILT, INNOCENCE, and the LAW

"I see. They pin it all on me."

—response to the sergeant in the Redlands drug bust, who said that any drug-taking at Keith's home will be his responsibility

"I don't think anyone who takes smack feels guilty about taking smack. What they're really guilty about is something else. Some of them want to feel guilty. They *need* to feel guilty. And smack is the best thing to take if you want to feel guilty about anything. It's the perfect excuse to feel guilty."

"I don't like to regret heroin—because I learned a lot from it. It was a large part of my life. It is something I went through and dealt with."

"People hate themselves anyway. If it wasn't smack, they'd hate themselves for eating carrots. You can bet on it."

"We're still the only rock 'n' roll band arrested for peeing on a wall."

"I just wondered if the uniform was with stripes or arrows."

—at the press conference following his
1978 court appearance for drugs, when
asked if he'd prepared for prison

"I could never think of music in terms of guilt. I've plcd guilty twenty-five times in a row, but not to music."

—on being asked if he has any
guilty pleasures in music

THE GUITAR

"Three notes, two fingers, and an asshole, and you've got it! You can play the darned thing. That's all it takes. What you do with it is another thing."

"They made me love them, but they beat me up bad."

—referring to the banged-up
condition of his hands

"It means I make the most noise."

—response to defense attorney's question
of what it means to play guitar, 1977

"At some time during the day you've gotta stroke the baby."

"You look at it, and it's a ... tennis racquet, but the more you find out about it, the more you don't know. Which is great because it means you've still got more to find out."

"Everybody should be born with a guitar—there'd be far less suicides."

"If I was suddenly stuck alone—I could probably stop myself from going mad as long as I had a guitar."

"The guitar, apart from its musical worth and versatility, also has a mystique about it ... that is very central to rock 'n' roll."

"The shape of the guitar is very feminine. There's many times I've slept with that thing."

"The reason I play it is that the more you do, the more you learn. I found a new chord the other day. I was like, 'Shit, if I had known that years ago ...' That's what's beautiful about the guitar. You think you know it all, but it keeps opening up new doors. I look at life as six strings and twelve frets. If I can't figure out everything that's in there, what chance do I have of figuring out anything else?"

HEALTH

"There's only one fatal disease, I've concluded. It's called hypochondria. And it's deadly."

"My epitaph will be: 'Fuckers! I told you I wasn't feeling well!' "

"Tours develop their own strains of bacteria and bugs. They make their own diseases."

"There have been great strides made in medical science lately. That's why I am able to say to you, 'Good evening, ladies and gentlemen. Welcome to the Rock and Roll Hall of Fame.' "

"I'm free of hypochondria—although I've got everything else."

"The idea that life is a regime, of trying to be this way or this, is ludicrous. Everyone is different, and I think everybody should take their lives and bodies in their own hands and get to know it. Mine likes to be abused, preferably by myself."

"You've only got to have one broken tooth for everyone to think you're a villain."

"You know the British Museum has one of those glass cases with my liver's name on it, and they're going to have to wait a long fucking time for it."

"I am very, very regular, I'll have you know. There are two things in this game—one's called bowel movement and the other's called vowel movement."

"I only get ill when I give up drugs."

HEROES

"The greats are the greats. You know who they are."

"None of the great ones ever sort of ... stop."

"There's a limit to hero worship."

"Me."

—when asked which historical figure he most identifies with

HISTORY

"There's got to be people around who know it all, man. Nobody ever really finds out what's important with the kinds of government you've got now. Fifty years after, they tell you what really went on. They'll let you know what happened to Kennedy in ... time ... They'll say who did it. But by then it won't matter; they'll all be dead and gone, and, 'Now it's different, and this more enlightened age ...' "

ILLUSION and IMAGE

"You could be sick as a dog, but as long as you've got a suntan, everybody thinks you're in great shape."

"When the lie doesn't work."

*—when asked what he dislikes
most about his appearance*

"I think photography is magic. It even made me look good a couple of times."

"An image is a great ball and chain to drag about. Now and again you play with it, and other times it becomes a weight, but I've gotten used to it."

"Because it's in black-and-white and because the camera wobbles, everybody thinks, Wow, this is for real, man, and all the time it was obviously set up ... It's so far removed from what actually goes on."

*—on the supposed documentary
film* Cocksucker Blues

"I used to pose in front of the mirror at home. I was hopeful. The only thing I was lacking was a bit of bread to buy an instrument. But I got the moves off first, and I got the guitar later."

"I try to feel ecstatic, and look ecstatic all the time."

"Guys that don't really know me, they're more likely to be the child of my image. Chasing an image is a dangerous game."

*—on the early death of Johnny
Thunders, Keith impersonator*

"It's very easy to end up being a parody of yourself."

"One Most Likely to Kick the Bucket ... I held that position for several years ... Sid Vicious beat me to it. Loads of others. That shows how wrong the charts can be."

INDEPENDENCE

"The minute you pay somebody to take care of [your image and independence] you might as well kiss it off. It's like buyin' a facade, you're not actually buying protection. You're buying what people think."

INDIVIDUALITY and IDENTITY

"I've desperately tried to remain anonymous. The state the world is in today, it's much more of an advantage to remain anonymous than it is to be identifiable or recognized."

"Because everybody has a different idea of who Mick Jagger is, he's confused himself now as to who he actually is ... It's a tremendous hassle to keep Mick in reality because he is so easily influenced." (SEE ALSO MICK)

"I had to stop doing Chuck Berry and start doing Keith Richards."

"Just be yourself is all I can say, the rest of it's a fucking joke."

"When I could play something, it was an added bright thing to my life. 'I've got that, if nothing else.' "

"I ain't gonna live in the box people want to put me in. That's their trip, not mine."

"The point is—who are you?"

"You've gotta be cool with yourself. If you've gotta think about being cool, you ain't cool."

"John Doe. There is no such person. There's no such thing as Mr. Average. Everybody's who they are. Feel it. Stay in touch with it."

"I can never remain anonymous—that's the reason why I've been picked up by the police so many times."

INNER DEMONS

"My policy is to identify one and deal with that."

"There is a demon in me, but I only own up to having one of them. Brian probably had forty-five ... He was so self-important, maybe because he was so short."

"[Brian] had so many hang-ups he didn't know where to hang himself ... So he drowned himself."

"Probably nobody knows how many demons they've got."

"There's a demon in everybody. It's the trying to express it—there's a dark piece in all of us.

—*referring to Muddy Waters and the*
nature of expressing the blues

"He's still around. Without the dope, we have a bit more of a chat these days. It's been more of a truce."

—*on that demon inside him*

INSPIRATIONS and INFLUENCES

"It was a bit of a shock, but it was a great one, like, shock me some more!"

—*on Little Richard*

"'A-wop-bop-a-loo-bop, a-lop-bam-boom.' For me, the world then went from black-and-white to Technicolor. Just like that—there it is! That's as concise as I can put it. It's the best bit of English I've ever heard."

"Little Richard, Elvis, Chuck Berry were all flying at me like an artillery barrage."

"Such a mixture of spoiled, moody brat and innocent, prolific artist."
—*on Chuck Berry*

"They were exactly what was needed. It was a great enema."
—*on the Beatles*

"They were just as filthy as we were."
—*on the Beatles*

"The Beatles kicked the doors open, and we zoomed in behind them."

"Phil is, was, and always will be a complete weirdo."
—*on Phil Spector*

"I nicked a lot off him. I took him for all he was worth. That's where you get 'Honky Tonk Women' from. His tuning, the fucking lot. I ripped him off."
—*on Ry Cooder*

"I just want to be Muddy Waters. Even though I'll never be that good or that black."

"The only guy I know who could make every chick in the audience weep ... Beautiful pain. He had that to the max."
—*on Gram Parsons*

"When you heard him, you knew that guy. Once touched, never forgotten."
—*on Gram Parsons*

"He was ... very similar to me in that he was trying to find his own place to hide. He just hid too deep."
—*on Jimi Hendrix*

"Gram Parsons ... Ian Stewart ... They still join the band when we're playing, in one form or another. You carry little shades of them with you."

"He's part of my staple diet. As necessary as vegetables are ... None of us are immortal, but if one of us is, it's gotta be that guy."

—on Jerry Lee Lewis

"I *want* a strong opening act. If they're good, it's going to make me work that much harder."

"It started for me when I first heard Little Richard and Elvis and Buddy Holly. Without that, there's no way we would be talking now."

"The amazing thing about Aretha is ... when she sings, she's chain-smoking. Dionne Warwick's another one. And they've both got these voices! Maybe I should smoke more!"

"He was in the union. One of the troubadours. He passed it on. Everything he did ... you still hear it on the radio today. He's in everybody. This is not bad for a guy from Lubbock."

—on Buddy Holly

"John Lee Hooker: He's seventy-eight, and he's got fifteen girlfriends. We should all be so lucky!"

INSTINCT

"The more you try to literally perfect them [songs], the more you lose the instinctive thing. Instinct is what I want."

"We work mostly by feel. I find it's better that way. I try not to think about it too much because I believe that people and their brains have probably screwed up enough things as it is, and rock 'n' roll is better left to instinct, you know."

JEALOUSY

"You have to fight all these young, aging, balding guys that are so jealous of that fact that you can do this shit and they wish you dead."

"People want to pull the rug out from under you, because they're bald and fat and can't move for shit. It's pure physical envy ... 'How dare they defy logic?'"

"We could have written all the jokes ourselves."

—in response to the cracks about the
Stones being over the hill

JUDGMENT

"You can't climb inside of somebody else's brain. Well, somebody climbed in mine once, but that was out of necessity."

KEITH RICHARDS

"I do what I do. Don't try this at home."

"There's been loads of wannabes. But it's all posing with a guitar. And not playing right, not looking right, so—not being me. It's amazing so many people would try to emulate me."

"To some, I'm a junkie madman who should be dead, and to others, I'm a mythical genius."

(SEE ALSO SANITY)

"I say good luck to people who want to emulate me, but they better realize what they're getting into; they better know that there's more to this than attitude. It's about the music; it's about the blues. That's what sustains me."

"If people want to be like Keith Richards, then they better have the same physical makeup. I come from a very sturdy stock—otherwise I wouldn't be there."

"I think I was born with the Keef riff, because to me it's 'Satisfaction' backwards, and I hear it in nearly every song that I do."

"Who'd want this blood?"

—in response to a question about his
rumored blood transfusion

"It's not that easy to be Keith Richards. But it's not so hard either."

"I can be the cat onstage anytime I want. I like to stay in touch with him ... But I'm a very placid, nice guy ... It's mainly to placate this other creature that I work."

"The things that would kill other people don't kill me. Despite everything, I'm a survivor. I can only suppose that I possess the kind of mentality and psychological makeup that could handle it."

"I don't look to go through life being someone else's image of Keith Richards. I know who he is. I'm inside him. The idea of partying for nine days in order to keep the image of Keith Richards up is stupid. That was Keith Richards then. Now I'll stay up just two or three days."

"I'm a Sagittarius, half-man, half-horse, with a license to shit in the street."

"I can be 'Keef' any time. That's easy. But there are other sides to me that are there for myself. I don't want to sound ungrateful, but that image—'I'm Keef and I'm stoned out of my mind all the time'—can be like a ball and chain. Now and again, I try to enlighten people that there is another side to it all."

"The bugger stuck electrodes all over my body, hooked up more monitors to me than the Stones use onstage, and told me I was— normal! I mean, can you imagine anyone telling Keith Richards he was normal?"

—on a trip to the doctor

"For me, the music is the important thing, and the image comes from the way I play it."

"I'm Baudelaire rolled in with a few other cats."

"Really, it's just in the bones and in the moves. You don't know what attracts people to what you do."

"I actually managed to turn my little juvenile fantasies into a way of life."

"I couldn't have written this story, man."

"Poor old cockroaches."

*—responding to the line that only
cockroaches and Keith Richards would
survive a nuclear holocaust*

KINDNESS

"It's important that people don't feel left out."

"The truth is, the more you give, the stronger you are."

LIFE and LIVING

"I'm doomed to live."

"Hey, you come and you go."

"In a way, I don't really mind all of the shit that I've had to go through. At least it kept me in touch with reality."

"I try to make things as simple and pure as possible, and have a great time."

"It's good to see you. In fact, it's good to see anyone."

"As far as I'm concerned, life is all you get and I'll make the best out of it ... I want to be here. And I want to see where I'm going."

"As Chekhov said, 'Any idiot will face a crisis, it's this day-to-day grind that'll get you down.' "

"It's the search that's important ... it doesn't matter if you're successful or famous ... it's that somebody picks up on it. That's the greatest epitaph: 'Rest in peace—he passed it on.' "

"The more you find out, the less you realize you know."

"All the crap you go through, I mean, how bad is it, really?"

LOVE

"Love wears a white Stetson."

"I say, out front, take it on or get out."

—on whether or not he's a hard man to love

"I'm a *lover*. I've been trying to tell people this for years."

—*responding to Marianne Faithfull's
assertion that sleeping with Keith
was the best night of her life*

"Nobody ever divorced *me*."

"One I do with the guitar and one I do without. But at least the guitar has a nice shape."

—*on being asked if making love and
playing a concert are similar*

MARKETING

"I don't really care what they write about us, so long as they write about us."

"I went to art school, which means I don't know shit about art but I know how to advertise."

"If they wrote about me as the sweet, gentle, loving family man, it would probably do me more damage. And be equally untrue."

"I'm the next Mickey Mouse—look out."

MATURITY

"I'm a late bloomer."

"It is all part of growing up. We promise that once we get mature, we'll go far."

"My dad said to me on his deathbed, 'We never stop growing ...' That was the last thing he said, and then I closed his eyes. He always said that younger people think older people know everything, but older people know they don't know shit from shit anyway."

"Nobody stops growing, otherwise there's no point in doing the trip in the first place."

MICK

"It's like a marriage with no divorce."

"The only things Mick and I disagree about is the band, the music, and what we do."

"I can get rid of my old lady. I can get rid of my kids. But I can't get rid of you."

—on the unending bond with his evil twin

"Mick would be nowhere without me. To me, Mick has only ever half-discovered his real potential."

"[Mick] can't go to sleep without writing out what he's going to do when he wakes up. I just hope to wake up, and it's not a disaster."

"He's my best friend. And my worst enemy."

"Creative tension? We rely on it!"

"You cut with Mick, your face is gonna look like mine. You may be Babyface now, but you're gonna be Fuckface like me after you get out of the studio with that guy!"

—advice to singer and producer Babyface

"Vanity will not carry a band. But a band can carry vanity."

"Mick *is* pretty good at business. He's not as good as people think. He's probably not as good as he thinks. And he's probably not as bad as *I* think."

"I'm always sorry for Mick's women, because they end up crying on my shoulder. And I'm like, 'How do you think *I* feel? I'm *stuck* with him.'"

"There's no possibility of divorce. We have to take care of the baby."
—on the inevitability of staying with Mick forever

"I understand the desperation of somebody like that, the insecurity that says, 'Until I am sure of myself I can't let anybody get too close, or I'll get really confused.'"

"What's so *hard* about being Mick Jagger? This exaggerated sense of who you are and what you should do and worrying about it so much. Why don't you just get on with it and stop trying to figure all the angles?"

"Mick is a weird mixture of people. He's still trying to live with 'em all."

"It's probably made him buckle down a bit more because he's being disapproved of ... We have other names for him apart from Sir."
—on Mick's knighthood

"I once saw Mick outside Dartford Library selling ice creams from a refrigerated trolley. Summer job. I hope he remembers the moves."
—in case he ever needs them again

"Mick has to get up with a plan ... Me, I wake up, praise the Lord, then make sure all the phones are turned off."

"With the Stones he's great. It's best to keep him on a short leash."

"If we were a mum-and-pop operation, then he'd be Mum."

"Mick's rock. I'm roll."

"What the hell would Mick do?"

—when asked why he doesn't sing more songs

"Mick is very good at being Mick."

"You're no Mick Jagger."

—to Mick Jagger

MONEY

"After one thousand pounds comes ten thousand pounds—and then after that it means nothing. It's just a lot of money. You don't think about it."

"I'd rather make it than talk about it."

"I've got enough to buy off questions I don't wanna answer."

—in response to the question of how much money he has

"But what does a millionaire do if he happens to spend over a million dollars a year? That makes him a pauper, you know. I could earn that title very quickly."

"A lot of our astute moves have been basically keeping up with tax laws, where to go, where not to put it."

"If this is a social call ... that's fine. If you're here to discuss how much money you're going to dredge from the European tour next year, then you can fuck off."

—to a Stones finance man

"The more money you make, the less you can afford."

MORTALITY

"Brushes with death are always, I've found, quite enervating in a way."

"Hitler thought that [he was indestructible] and eventually had to kill himself."

"That's the dichotomy between this planet and ourselves. We own it, we think. So did the dinosaurs, at one time, and look what happened to them."

"Other people's shopping doesn't interest me."

—on being told he was on Mark Chapman's
1980 hit list, along with John Lennon

MOVING ON

"I've recently retired from military combat and I don't want no more to do with fighting."

"The bus is still rolling ... You can't get off this machine, except when the wheels fall off."

"I don't sit in trees anymore."

MUSIC and CREATIVITY

"All music is holy."

"Music's meaning to people is one of the great mysteries."

"Music is a language that doesn't speak in particular words. It speaks in emotions, and if it's in the bones, it's in the bones."

"It's just the stuff to play it on that is a luxury."

"The album is called *Talk Is Cheap* because if we were able to talk about music, there would be no need for music. Music performs a function that can only be provided by the very fact that it is music ... A function that is totally separate from anything else."

"How long has this human race been around? We don't even know, right? They keep finding that we're older than we thought. The first music probably came from a guy beating on a rock. 'Here comes a tiger.' That's your first beat. 'Warning.' "

"I hate to see music being used as propaganda. But then I think back and realize it always has been—national anthems and signaling. Music started out as a signaling process. When it comes down to it, music evolved out of necessity, not out of pleasure. Somebody got lucky, whipped the other tribe's ass, and then they could use music for fun for a little while because there's no competition. You get the rockin' down: 'We won, we won.' You start to get those songs coming in, apart from just the signaling. And after that, there's this progression."

"I love my kids most of the time, and I love my wife most of the time. Music I love all the time. It's the only constant thing in my life. It's the one thing you can count on."

"Certain sounds can kill. It's a specialty of the French for some reason. The French are working with huge great speakers which blow down houses and kill laboratory technicians with one solitary blast."

"My music is about chaos. Nothing happens quite when you think it's supposed to or when you want it to, but when it does, you've got to roll with it ... It slams you the wrong way here, and then suddenly it's in the right place ... just like life."

"Good music comes out of people playing together, knowing what they want to do and going for it. You have to sweat over it and bug it to death. You can't do it by pushing buttons and watching a TV screen."

"Is it just a distraction or is it a vision or God knows what? It's everything to all kinds of people."

"Every sound has an effect on the body, and the effects of a good backbeat makes these people shiver in their boots, so you are fighting some primeval fear that you can't even rationalize, because it's to do with the chromosomes and the exploding genes."

"We're only alive because the heart *beat* keeps going on all the time."

"I call it 'marrow music.' It's beyond the bone."

—on Rastafarian chanters

"Imagine if Mozart and Beethoven had a fucking Walkman! You wouldn't have had twenty-six overtures, you'd have fifty-bleeding-nine. Those guys would be green with envy. They would burn their wigs."

"Basically any beat that you've got on this continent comes from Africa. The climate and the people controlling your area—Spanish, French, or English—would determine from there on which way it would go ... any music from the islands or Latin America is from Africa. It's the predominant tribal beat of that area ... Just another manifestation of the movement of rhythm and harmony and melody over the face of the planet. That's what counts."

"I've seen people physically throw up from feedback in the studio. It's so loud it started their stomach walls flapping. But on another level, if you go to Africa or Jamaica, you see people living to that rhythm. It's magic in that it's an unexplored area."

"I can give you the history of the world—just give me their music."

"Give me a tribe's music, and I'll tell you how they live, what they smell like ... almost. That would give me more information than talking to them or looking at 'em."

"Every sound ... vibration has a certain effect on you. You can make certain noises that automatically make you throw up. And there is nothing you can do about it."

"Music is a necessity, because it's the one thing that will maybe bring you up and give you just that little bit extra to keep on going."

"It takes certain mysterious cycles for things to come together to produce consistently good music."

"There's something about music. When you like it, you want to find out where it came from."

"You don't have to be a fucking star. Music is something from your own heart for your own home."

MUSIC and its SOCIAL and POLITICAL IMPACT

"Music's the best communicator ... And I doubt anybody would disagree ... that some major shifts in superpower situations in the last few years has an awful lot to do with the last twenty years of music, or just music in general. It's like the walls of Jericho again."

"You can build a wall to stop people, but eventually, the music, it'll cross that wall. There's no defense against it. I mean, look at Joshua and fuckin' Jericho—made *mincemeat* of that joint. A few trumpets, you know."

"Why should rock 'n' roll music suddenly appear in the mid-fifties, catch hold, and just get bigger and bigger and show no signs of abating?"

"The music business, in any given year, is ninety-eight percent crap. If you know that, and can avoid the posing ... you might fail totally 'making it' ... but it's not going to hurt you to go for that two percent. But go for the other ninety-eight and you're lost."

"[Music] is why the iron curtain went down. It was jeans and rock 'n' roll that took that wall down in the long run. It wasn't all those atomic weapons and that facing down and big bullshit. What finally crumbled it was the fuckin' music, man. You cannot stop it. It's the most subversive thing."

"Forget economics, forget democracy or dictatorships or monarchies. The most fascinating relationship is between people and music and how it can do what it does with no apparent sweat. Who knows what it can do? It's a beautifully subversive language because it can get through anything. I don't care if it's porous or bombproof or has a *Star Wars* shield over it—music will get through. That's my experience."

"Country music comes quite naturally—after all, those melodies basically originate in England, Wales, Scotland, and Ireland ... it's just that the studs and rhinestones are hard to find in England!"

"I can't believe that a government would spend two seconds of its time worrying about what rock 'n' roll band is coming to its country. But they do."

"It's insinuated its way into the culture of every country in the world. It's one of the most subversive hidden forces. Nobody can control it."

"There were times when it was like the Stones were holding a gun at the head of the world. Other times, it felt like the other way round."

MUSICIANSHIP

"This stuff relies on muscle and sweat and the human touch. The music I play needs energy and power; I'm just trying to make it grow up a little within its parameters."

"Do you want a miracle, every fucking day? We work the way we work. It's none of your fucking business whether it's slow or fast. Get the fuck out! What do you mean, 'dead slow'? Did anybody moan at Beethoven how long it took him to write?"

—on being told the Stones
record music "dead slow"

"You always want to check out what the local cats are doing. And what goes in must come out, in one way or another. You have to be careful what you listen to, if you want to write songs."

"I'm very wary of trying to please other musicians."

"Any band that doesn't play live is only half a band as far as I'm concerned."

"I love playing the piano. It's nice to sit down on the job occasionally."

"You have to start very young to do this and then hope to stay alive."

"I would do it as a hobby even if I was an accountant now. And would probably be better off."

NEIGHBORS and OTHER PEOPLE

"I have a knack for finding a whole building of very cool people, you know, but there'll be one uncool couple, they're always a couple. And my apartment will always be either just above them or next door to them or just below ... 'We can't even hear Bugs Bunny on our TV, your music's so loud.' I'm plagued by that kind of thing."

"You learn to take people as they come. It doesn't matter where they come from. So you learn to size up people really quickly. If you don't you get into trouble."

NIGHT

"I've nothing against daylight. I don't live totally nocturnally. Only when I feel like it. Which is most of the time."

"I love this breakfast thing. It's a novelty to me."

> —*speaking at his man-of-the-
> year breakfast ceremony*

"Who said I get out of bed in the morning? The sheer joy of [music] is what gets me up at night."

> —*when asked what gets him out
> of bed in the morning*

"The permanent night shift."

> —*what Keith calls his body's
> attunement to the night*

"It doesn't swagger so much in the morning."

> —*when asked how much the swaggering
> character is the real Keith Richards*

"How many dawns do most people see? They really miss out. After a nice long night, it's the most beautiful part of the day."

NOSTALGIA

"Nostalgia is a luxury."

"I think you probably get more nostalgic the older you get. But not to the point where I can say, 'I really wanna drive up and see the old school where I was expelled from.'"

"We're not on a nostalgia trip. We're not playing for people who remember when they got laid to one song in the sixties. We're trying to connect then with now and keep going."

OPTIMISM

"My guitar is tuned, and I'm ready to go."

"I'm ready to rock."

"I'll just keep on rocking and hope for the best."

ORIGINALITY

"I start to feel good about records when I realize I can toss away the rule book."

OUTCASTS and OUTLAWS

"Sometimes I sway between being a prisoner and an outcast. I'm not sure whether they're keeping me in or pushing me out."

PASSING IT ON

"What Muddy Waters did for us is what we should do for others."

"I find it very heartening for myself that I get a lot of stuff from thirteen-, fourteen-year-old would-be guitar players, because my theory is that the only thing you can put on a musician's headstone is, 'He passed it on.' So personally that makes me feel very warm."

"Brother, you've made your deal now. The only thing you can do is pass it on ... That's for the tombstone, baby: 'He passed it on.' "

THE PAST

"You uncover fragments of the past every time you think back. It's like a broken mirror. And every now and again you get a glimpse of what happened."

PATRIOTISM

"I don't wave a flag for anything. I'm a musician."

"You'll never get rid of nationalism and so-called patriotism, but the important thing is to spread the idea that there's really this one planet—that's what we've really to worry about."

"I got expelled from school, why not get expelled from your own country?"

"We just carry Britain with us, really, our little bubble of it."

"They're going through their little traumas over there [England]. It serves them right for kickin' us out."

PIRATES

"Both are ways to make a good dishonest living."

—on rock stars and pirates

"Pirates are very democratic. Everything's for sale: left leg so much, testicles so much. I mean, they did have a deal going on those boats that was way ahead of the Constitution."

"If I didn't have a guitar, I'd have a boat."

"The rest of the Stones are kicking their asses back, and I'm a pirate."

—on his role in The Pirates of Caribbean

"Shit, I'll do anything. How difficult is it for me to play a pirate? Just stick a hat on me and a beard. But it's not necessary to wear all that stuff to be a pirate. Most pirates these days wear suits."

"You should see who I've modeled myself on. Unfortunately, he's somewhere up there. He's so great, he's invisible."

—referencing Depp's modeling his
Pirates *character on Keith, and Keith*
then playing Johnny's father

POISON

"Poison's not bad. It's a matter of how much."

(SEE ALSO DRUGS)

POLICE, THE LAW, and INCARCERATION

"Police ... are basically in the business of crime ... There's criminals, and there's police, but they're in the same business. They think the same way. If there is a criminal mentality, there has got to be a police mentality and it has got to be pretty much the same, since they are in the same business. It's not different than a wholesaler and a retailer in dealing in the same product. It's crime ... But it's still the same job. It's big business."

"The way they run the police force? The leader of a tribe of Boy Scouts has better intelligence ... They find a little paper bag under the couch and go, 'Gotcha!' "

"No matter how much they go in with their little speeches, it's still like a tennis match where the ball never stops."

—on courtrooms

"Going to court is just an expensive habit."

"When I am thrown in a court, or anybody like myself is thrown in court, the jury has got absolutely no experience in the musician's way of life, so they're not your peers. I know justice is often rough and so on, but they don't know what it's like to be on the road for twenty years, and I can't explain it to them now. So ... give me a jury of my peers, with Chuck Berry, with Muddy Waters. And put Ron in there too. I mean, I can drop him a few bucks."

"They've had a go with trying. If they try again, I don't see any real way they can get away with it, just because they have been trying to get me and it never works."

—when asked if he's worried that the
law and police will finally get him

"I kept very much face-to-face with reality, mainly in the shape of a judge or policeman. That kind of worked, as an anchor, sort of brought me down to everybody else's level, really, because I was made very aware that as far as they were concerned, I was a piece of shit that they wanted to see behind bars."

POLITICS

"Politics is an ugly word these days, and the only people who make politics an ugly word are politicians, because they are ugly people."

"How many times can you use those words—justice, freedom. It's like margarine, man. You can package it and you can sell that too. In America they have a great talent for doing that."

"Politics are what we were trying to get away from in the first place."

"It's an ongoing soap opera of the worst kind, but people still watch it."

"I never find it a happy marriage. It's like church and state."
—on leaving politics out of art

"I ... firmly believed Scotland Yard was incorruptible. Until I had to pay out ten grand and then get popped. And the scales fell from my eyes."

"It only takes one person to create a power struggle."
—referring initially to Mick

"I've always felt more sexual than political. I could never get that worked up about Edward Heath."

"I don't think rock 'n' roll music is at its fullest when it gets too involved with politics and tries to preach and say, 'You must do this,' or, 'You free him.' I think rock 'n' roll's real power is far more under the surface."

PREDICTIONS

"I hate predictions—they never turn out when I make them."

THE PRESENT

"The Rolling Stones have always believed in the present."

"Now."

—when asked what his idea of perfect happiness is

"Today's what counts."

THE PRESS

"Then don't be offensive."

—in response to a journalist asking a question about his clothes with the disclaimer "I don't mean to be offensive"

"That question you just asked me."

—when asked by a journalist which question he is asked most often

PRISON

"First off, neither the accommodations nor the fashion suited me at all. I like a little more room, I like the john to be in a separate area, and I hate to be woken up. The food's awful, the wine list is terribly limited, and the library is abysmal."

"The first thing you do automatically when you wake up is drag the chair to the window and look up to see what you can see out the window. It's an automatic reaction. That one little square of sky, trying to reach it."

"The only point of sending someone on a drug bust to jail is to rehabilitate them. As I've done that myself, there shouldn't be any need for jail."

QUITTING

"The last time? ... Why the fuck should this be the last time? What else are we going to do? Get a job in an ad agency?"

"Yes, and the next five."

—when asked if this is the last tour

RACE

"Probably we all come from Africa. We just went north and turned white."

"If you cut anybody open, bones is white and blood is red, man ... Ancient marrow responding to the source. All it points out is the superficiality of racial differences."

"To me, the other side of the tracks is where I can really rest."

"I like hanging out with black people. It's so much easier. They think I'm one anyway, I'm just in disguise."

"I've always felt that there's a slight racial bias ... If I was black, nobody would go on about how old I was. They'd say, 'Wonderful that he's still going.' They wouldn't go on about thinning hairlines and wrinkles and all that crap."

REBELLION

"I think a lot of this 'rebel' thing has been brought up by people thinking too much about it. People like you come up to us and say, 'Are you rebels?' The answer is no."

REGRET

"I don't regret nothin'."

"The one thing I don't wanna do is quit early and then sit around for the rest of my life wondering what would have happened had I carried on. That would be a regret and I don't like them."

"I know I didn't do nothin' wrong."

RELIGION and SPIRITUALITY

"If you're looking for a guru, forget it—they find you, you don't find them."

"A guru looks for his fucking apprentice. One day somebody'll tap me on the shoulder and it'll be a bloke in a turban saying, 'You!' and until that happens, I'll forget it. You know, I've too much else to take care of."

"I am quite proud that I never did go and kiss the Maharishi's goddamn feet, you know."

"If someone is involved in what's going on around them, they aren't gonna get caught up by a bunch of *Indian* hustlers."

"I have to draw the line at swamis."

"I read the Bible sometimes, but it bores me to death. I just want to know what other people find so bloody fascinating. Why are they all hung up on all that 'In the beginning' stuff? Ah, well. At least life is stable. It has said the same thing since I was a kid."

"Spirit is all around me. Very much. But mine is a very nebulous spirituality. I wouldn't care to put a name on it. I don't want to place any bets. [game-show-host voice] 'Oh, you picked the wrong god. Sorry, it's Allah.'"

"Religion is like Las Vegas. Placing bets on something. I prefer to take the larger point of view. Hey, give thanks and praises, whoever you are, wherever you are, whatever you are."

"We're the only form of life on this planet that needs religion, that will actually kill each other over some abstract idea."
(SEE ALSO ART)

"He never rehearses."

> —on God (whom he claims joins the band
> onstage via rain, wind, and snow)

"I love God. But I hate preachers."

"Leave that stuff at home when you come to see me."

> —regarding people who
> continuously talk about God

REPUTATION

"I'll gladly hand the title over to someone else. I'll even put an ad in the paper: NEW DRUG SCAPEGOAT REQUIRED FOR POSITION OF INTERNATIONAL FAME. It's all yours, buster."

"Of course I'm concerned about his reputation. I'm trying to save his reputation."

> —regarding Mick's accusations that
> Keith was jealous of the reputation
> he earned from his knighthood

"You drag your whole life behind you."

"Even though that was nearly twenty years ago, you cannot convince some people that I'm not a mad drug addict. So I've still got [that image] in my baggage."

"You tend to drag around your reputation as a kind of ball and chain—a long shadow."

THE RIDICULOUS and the SUBLIME

"You try saying twenty-five times, 'Guilty, your honour,' and keep a straight face."

THE ROAMING LIFE

"You can travel and move and still keep a family together. Otherwise there wouldn't have been gypsies and nomads."

"I don't think a constant hands-on thing with families is necessary, as long as you know where the heart lies. They can always find me and I can always find them."

"I don't know if anybody's better off from having their dad come home at exactly six o'clock every evening and disappear again at seven the next morning."

"For me an extended period of time is three weeks."

"The no-man's-nomad. The nomad's nomad."

—on describing his life of exile
and having no real home

ROCK 'N' ROLL

"Rock 'n' roll: Music for the neck downwards."

"Rock 'n' roll's great weapon is humor."

"Rock 'n' roll has lasted because nothing else came along."

"The rock's easy. But the roll is another thing."

"The biggest cliché in rock 'n' roll is there's no roll. They forgot the roll and they only kept the rock. The roll's the whole damn thing. The roll is king. Unfortunately most cats don't get behind the roll."

" 'Roll' means to be light and heavy at the same time. A feather touch. And that's what nobody really wants to know about, because it's too difficult to learn ... I think we should actually go to a university just for the roll."

"We didn't perceive the subversive power of rock 'n' roll, that it carried the seeds of something far more powerful ... Rock music became a political and social force. Maybe rock ' n' roll had more to do with breaking down Eastern Europe than anybody really wants to give credit for."

"Rock 'n' roll doesn't die—it matures."

"It's like wine, man, they just get better."

—on musicians as they get older

"Even when I was a kid, what I really loved about good rock 'n' roll was the maturity of it."

"Rock 'n' roll is really about interaction. It's not about the actual notes and chords, and it's not about just pushing buttons and letting machines do all the work ... it's really about the interesting tension and communication going on between one guy and another."

"That's one of the great things about rock 'n' roll—every night there's a different world's greatest band."

"I don't think rock 'n' roll should be analyzed or even thought about deeply. Hesitate, and you're lost."

"We never did anything consciously to shock people. All we ever did was answer the call of nature."

"It was almost like A.D. and B.C., and 1956 was year one ... The world was black-and-white, and then suddenly it went into living color. Suddenly there was a reason to be around."

"Rock 'n' roll is really a small-room thing. Over the years, we've had to learn to do it bigger. It just keeps getting bigger and bigger. It's like some kind of Frankenstein's monster, some huge juggernaut. And you can end up working for it, rather than it working for you. It can get so fucking big you can't do what you want to do anymore. That's why the Beatles stopped."

"I used to like it when TV and rock 'n' roll didn't get along. To me, TV is the family and the house. Rock 'n' roll is something outside the house."

"You should never underestimate the importance of country in rock 'n' roll."

"They are really out to make rock 'n' roll illegal."

"Rock 'n' roll got me into being one of the boys. Before that I just got me ass kicked all over the place. Learned how to ride a punch."

"I thought rock 'n' roll was an unassailable outlet for some pure and natural expression of rebellion. It used to be one channel you could take without ever havin' to kiss ass, you know?"

"You've got the sun, you've got the moon, you've got the air you breathe, and you've got the Rolling Stones."

"The music is bigger than all of us. What are we? We're just players, no matter how good."

"We're the Rolling Stones. No one tells us what to do. We'll stop when we feel like it."

"There's myriad ideas and concepts of what the Stones are ... just depending on how long they've known us. We're constantly going forward as well, always looking for the Stones in the same way. Sometimes you screw it up, but most times it gives us some encouragement that we'll find it again. It's very much a focused band, a lot of direction and energy. You can't ask for more than that."

"When it comes down to the nugget ... this thing is bigger than both of us. You cannot deny the Rolling Stones."

"This is basically Stu's band. We're working for a dead man."

*—on "sixth Stone" Ian Stewart, who
was taken out of the lineup early on to be
road manager, following his death*

"Playing live with the Stones is like living in your own separate country. It's like having an empire but no land."

"It's actually reached a point where probably a good eighty percent of the people there at the concerts don't even know a world without the Rolling Stones. And so you become a fixture—like the moon."

"Sometimes when you're in the dressing room before going on, you look around and think, *there's Mick, there's Charlie, there's Ron* ... There's me. And you suddenly think, is that all there is? Where's the one that knows everything?"

"How to turn football stadiums into bars has been our quest."

"At our best, we master the art of going just over the edge of the abyss, then pulling back."

"God joins the goddamn band every night in the form of wind, rain, and lightning."

"I don't see an end to the Rolling Stones. I don't think about it happening. When it comes, if it comes, whenever. Besides, it's all science fiction anyway."

"We breed our own viruses."

—talking about life on the road

"The Stones got too big, really, for what the Stones wanted to be."

"My gut reaction was that nobody leaves the band, except in a coffin. Mick Taylor was lucky … because he's not the sort of guy that you want to beat up."

"He turned us into … a sort of conspiracy."

—on Andrew Loog Oldham

"It's not easy to get into the Stones. It's even harder to leave."

"We've become Frank Sinatra."

RON WOOD

"Ronnie's a great mixture of talent and bullshit."

"Ronnie … never looks on the dark side of life, and sometimes you'll be thinking, 'Shut up, Ronnie, we don't want to be happy.' "

"You want a psychiatrist, go see Ronnie. He's a one-man suicide line. I could make a fortune selling tickets. Suicide court!

They'd come out laughing their heads off, with a new vision of life."

"I can never remember Ronnie pulling a gun on me. He wouldn't know which end to point."

"I've known him as stoned out of his brain ... and I've known him straight sober. And quite honestly, there's very little difference."

"Ronnie after all is the new boy—he's only been in the band twenty-seven years."

"I think being straight will suit him ... for a while."

"They could be burying him and he'd be laughing."

SANITY

"It's only people who are insane who think they're not."

"I'd never discourage a bunch of guys and girls getting together to play music. It's the one thing that may retain their sanity."

"Listening to music is an art; it can keep your sanity."

SCHOOL

"The nearest thing I been to it is Wormwood Scrubbs [prison]. Really, it's the same feeling."

"How could you *do* this to me, Marlon? I haven't been in a principal's office for thirty years."

> —*on finding out he had to go to his son Marlon's*
> *school following some trouble Marlon got in*

SELF-KNOWLEDGE

"I've lived my life in my own way, and I'm here because I've taken the trouble to find out who I am."

"The only thing I can say is, you gotta know yourself."

"People should check in with what's in here [the heart] and then see how you can deal with what's out there."

"I've come to a conclusion after many, many years of not knowing what the hell I'm doing: It's to just do it."

"Dealing with those kind of people taught me how to be not like them, taught me how to be a gentleman."

—on drug dealers

"I've lived my life in my own way, and I'm here today because I have taken the trouble to find out who I am."

"You can worry all you like. I'm not."

—in response to a reporter telling him he was worried about Keith's excessive habits

"I do think a certain amount of self-knowledge would help people, rather than being always distracted by exteriors."

"Hey, you can screw up. I have. Life doesn't get any easier as you get older. It just becomes more complex. At the same time, one starts to discern certain threads which are important to follow."

"Just to put yourself up on that stage, you've got to have an enormous ego. It's what you do with it in your spare time."

"The biggest mistake in the world is to think that you have to emulate somebody else."

"Boredom? To me, that's an illness. You could lock me up in solitary for weeks on end and I'd keep myself amused."

"You don't know me. I know me."

"The people who've told me to stop doing this and that and they've croaked ... I've had about three doctors who told me, 'If you carry on like this, you will be dead in six months.' I went to their funerals."

"All these gadgets now—it's all about anything to defy the interior, to defy dealing with yourself."

SELF-TRUST

"I didn't ask to be an example to other people ... All I know is myself. And I am the only one I can actually trust. I have many, many friends and I trust them a lot of the way down the line, but when it comes to life and death, I am the only one I can trust."

"I don't really have to promise myself anything. That's all part of the wonderfulness that is me. Like they say in America, 'If it ain't broken, then don't fix it.' "

—when asked what his
New Year's resolutions are

"I've always done things on a very instinctive basis. I think brains have gotten in the way of too many things."

"I'd rather take someone on face value and totally screw up."

SHOW BUSINESS

"My first taste of show business: when my voice broke and they didn't want me in the choir anymore. Suddenly it was, 'Don't call us, we'll call you.' I think that was when I stopped being a good boy and started to be a yob."

"The art of it is to create, for two hours, your own country, Stonesland—for you and several hundred thousand people."

"Rock 'n' roll bands normally play in garages, clubs, bars, and juke joints. Try and translate that into a football stadium."

"If you can't do it in a small joint, you ain't gonna do it in a big one."

"They can see how many spots you've got and how many teeth are left and whether your eyeballs are pinned. That's all over in the first few minutes, so then it's just a matter of them enjoying themselves."

—on audiences in small venues

"It's hard being out front. You gotta actually believe that you're semidivine when you're out there, then come off stage and know you ain't. And that's the problem: Eventually the reaction time gets slower. You still think you're semidivine when you're in the limo and semidivine at the hotel, until you're semidivine for the whole goddamn tour."

—on singers

"My one worry is falling over onstage."

"When you play onstage you're so conscious of it that you try to forget and just concentrate on playing. You try to ignore the audience as much as possible. If you think too much about the audience, you will just dry up and paralyze yourself."

"I'd rather the Mafia than Decca."

"It's rare that we do an American tour when someone doesn't die."

"I go onstage to get some fucking peace and quiet."

"Laundry."

*—relating the biggest problem
of being on the road*

SLEEP (and/or LACK OF IT)

It's part of the "laboratory experiment" of life—where your body is an instrument and you can set it at different levels and numbers. Altered states made easy.

"It's the most amazing experience. You lose track of time after three nights. An hour becomes a minute. A minute can become an hour. Time's meaningless, sleep becomes superfluous. Everything becomes a beautiful blur, until you fall over and break your nose."

—on the art of staying awake for days

"When you sleep, everything is so neatly put into compartments of that day and that day, and I did that on that day, but if you stay up for five or six days, the memory goes back into one long period with no breaks at all, and the days don't mean anything anymore."

"Nine [days of no sleep] was as far as I could go. And loads of four and fives ... But after three days, another thing clicks in. It's a fascinating world ... It was a laboratory. As far as I was concerned, the whole thing was a scientific expedition."

"Life was so interesting for nine days that I couldn't give it up. Not even for a minute."

—on staying awake for nine days

SOCIETY

"Everything's run on a shoestring, including society."

"If you can get along with one person, then it's gotta be possible that everybody can get along with everybody. Somehow."

"If they hadn't come smashing through my front door, no one would've known what example I was setting."

—on being a bad example for society

"As long as you don't feel isolated and completely cut off from everything, you're okay."

SONGWRITING
(see also WRITING and INVENTION)

"Songs are funny things. They wake you in the middle of the night and say, 'I go like this.' Once you've started them off, you're not in control of them. They control you. They're like precocious little children. 'Now I wanna go here ... Now you put this on me ...' You humor them until they come out right."

"I don't think I write 'em, I think I receive 'em."

"Throughout the years, certain songs have screamed out, 'I want to go onstage!' With others, it was more like, 'Remember me?' And they'd get trampled."

"I'm almost to the point now, after writing songs for so many years, that there is only one song—it's just the variations you come up with. It sometimes seemed that there was only one song, and that was 'Satisfaction.' "

"I'd let the rest of the best think that I know what I'm doing. I'll just start playing. And I'll rely on my intuition and instinct."

"Songs do weird things. They grow as you play them over the years ... The thing is just barely out of the womb and then you play it for like thirty years. You realize that was the baby you put on record, and it's still growing every time you play it. As simple as they appear to be, there's so many things that you learn about them. You say, 'Ah, I wish I had put this or that on the original.' "

"I never think a song is finished being written just because you've recorded it and put it out. Now it can grow, because other people are going in to hear it. That's when it takes on its real meaning."

"Nobody talked to me for six months because they all thought it was all about them."

—on the song "All About You"

"They think they're God. And that's a very bad mistake!"

—regarding the overly high self-regard of songwriters

"Songs, to me, come through osmosis ... all the best songs are basically beautiful accidents. It happens very suddenly. So it's just a matter of recognizing it when it comes."

"To me, writing songs is like making love: You need two to write a song."

"I love it when they drip off the end of the fingers."

"My ten favorite discs? That's the toughest question of all, like, Is there a God?"

"Songwriting is such a mystery to me as it is to anyone else. I mean, the best songs to me are the ones I write in bed. That means I don't even have to move. The guitar's always next to the bed, the tape recorder's always next to the bed ... that's luxury to me!"

"I can't write a note of music, but then neither could most of the best songwriters of the last fifty years."

"I go through a lot of what we call 'vowel movement,' when you get in front of a microphone and forget what the hell the song is supposed to be about, and just start to sing, *eee, oooo, aaah* ... You let the vowels fit in with the track and add the consonants later, and they become the words ... The song will form itself around the vowel movement. A regular vowel movement. We like that in a band."

"If you try and add a melody to a riff rather than it evolving from it, it always sounds completely false, like the melody's been stuck on the top with a piece of cellotape."

"They usually disappear of their own accord. That's the thing about songs—you don't have to be scared of them dying. They keep poking you in the face."

"I don't know. You tell me."

—when asked what the best
song is that he's written

STAGE FRIGHT

"I think stage fright is a luxury. If you want to play to people, you know you'll overcome it. If the idea of standing out there is going to make you sick, you'd better not do it or you'll get ulcers. There is a bit of show-off in us all, and you'd better nurture that if you want to stand out on a stage in front of a hundred thousand people."

"If you can get through one show, you can get through hundreds."

STARTING OUT

"They looked at us like we were martians. Complete strangers, and they all hated us and wanted to beat the shit out of us."

"We'd seen all the screaming chicks ... and couldn't wait to hear them scream for us."

—on seeing the Beatles

"We went to a gig and then a riot started and the kids hit the stage and the only big deal was how the hell are we getting out ... climbing over the rooftops with chief constables who don't know their way ... getaways down fire escapes, through laundry chutes, and into bakery vans. We ended up being like the Monkees without even realizing it."

"A recording contract ... as remote as God talking to you."

STRENGTH and SUFFERING ... and WALKING THROUGH the FIRE

"At the end of the day you don't mess with me. There's no point in doing it."

"I wanted to come back and prove that what I had gone through had made a difference, to justify this kind of suffering."

"Heroin ... It's a mug's game, just because of the things you have to go through to get it. But when you're off it, it's a fucking comedy, really. Once you've been through it and out the other end, then you can afford to laugh at it. It's only when you don't make it out the other end that, y'know, you can't laugh at anything."

"The strong guys are gentle, always. It's only weak guys that come on strong."

"I said to myself, 'Okay, the experiment will now come to an end. This is a laboratory, and we're closing the laboratory down.' "

SUPERSTITION

"I never went in for superstition."

"Nobody wants to go near something that has a jinx on it. But you have to take the jinx off, take the voodoo away, and have another look."

SURVIVAL and BOUNCING BACK

"I don't think about surviving. I just expect it."

"You know, I got a feeling this town's gonna make it."

—to a New York City audience
at a 9/11 tribute concert

"Cold turkey is not so bad after you've done it ten or twelve times."

"If surviving means getting old, yeah, I'm a survivor."

"Everybody wants to make like, 'Oh, I've been to hell and back.' You've only been halfway. Nobody's been there and back."

"I've been in car crashes where ... I've watched it from above, saying, 'This is it. No way am I going to survive ...' You just disappear and suddenly when it's time for you to be back inside yourself ... you're there."

"The answer is not to keep asking yourself how you do it. As long as you do it. I don't try to analyze it."

—when asked how he continues on

"Once you've survived a Liverpool or London crowd, you can take care of yourself anywhere in the world."

"Doctors all over the world want my body when it finally goes. Apparently I do have an incredible immune system. I had hepatitis C and cured it by myself. Just by being me."

"What's so hard? What's so difficult? Everyone has struggles in their life. I had a baby die. Been busted, threatened with jail and death and all kinds of things. But ... who hasn't, in one form or another? That's life. It was other people's projections that I was at death's door ... That's why I'm still here. Really, number one on the list? Look out, cock, I'll be around!"

"I've only fallen over twice in fifteen gigs. But still kept playing."

TALENT

"Everybody has a talent. But how many get to find what their talent is before they're sucked into the system? I mean, it usually ends up as their hobby, which is probably what they're really good at ... They're working their guts out doing something they don't really like to do ... and at night they go home and on the weekends they have a hobby. They are working to get those few hours to spend on their hobby, when that's the area they should really be working in ... If you get to find out what your talent is before you're sucked into doing something you don't want to do ... that's the big fuck-up. If people were doing things they really wanted to do, they'd do it ten times better."

TECHNOLOGY

"Cellular phones ... It's like sticking your head in a microwave oven ... Alexander damn Graham Bell, I'd shoot him."

"Synthesizers and the Internet are things that really should have been kept secret."

"The thing that strikes me as strange is that as more and more possibilities present themselves, the more records sound alike, and I think that's wrong. Technology is supposed to be a tool that widens the spectrum to make more possibilities available, but ... it is working negatively."

"The way they deliver a record is with some seminude chicks. The music becomes like elevator background music. Andy Warhol's little dream's come true. Everybody's a star for fifteen minutes."

—on the MTV generation

"I'd say that nearly every rock 'n' roll band spends at least fifty percent of their time in the studio trying to dirty up the sound—in other words, trying to fight the technology ... Everybody knows that the best rock 'n' roll records were made with one mike in a tiny room."

TIME

"What is life but playing with time?"

"Maybe age does matter, in that you consider time a different way. You start to use it more, rather than clambering all over it and using it as scaffolding."
(SEE ALSO AGING)

"I'm timeless now, I'm beyond time."

"The end of the century is always weird because people go berserk about the zeros. For some reason there's a mass psychosis. In the 1890s they were mad, too, you know."

"I'm sixty, am I? I knew it was one of those with a zero on the end."

"Have you noticed that Einstein was right, that time is relative?"

TRAVELING

"The first thing you need to do with a hotel room is to stop it looking like a hotel room. It's a ministage, right? My big luxury is carrying a big stereo—about three cases full of sound. I couldn't live without that cushion of sound."

"I like to see the way the world's going round."

TROUBLE

"The mundane has never interested me particularly."

"It's not that I look for trouble. It's more an electromagnetic thing. I seem to attract it. I'm waiting for the next hit."

TRUTH

"The only way I've ever been able to survive any of this crap is by saying, 'Anything you put on your front page, I can top it.' Because I'll give you the real lowdown, which is far more interesting."

"I don't want anybody to think it's worth snooping around in my backyard thinking they're gonna pick up anything that they wouldn't learn by asking me."

"I'd rather look people in the eye when I'm talking to them. Unless it's an important message, like, 'Get the hell out of there, the cops are coming.'"

"I was kind of forced into the position of honesty because they went through my garbage cans and it was all over the front pages."

"I've got nothing to hide. Nothing's a state secret with me."

"I have nothing to hide. I found that's the best way to get along with everybody."

"Hunter S. Thompson."

—when asked to name his favorite fictional hero—citing the "truth-telling" journalist

"The press turn you into what they want you to be, and as far as the people are concerned, that's what you are."

"My big mouth put me on the spot many times. But I know at times there are things that need to be said, it doesn't matter where it is and who it's said to. Sometimes I can hear myself talking and saying, 'You should keep your mouth shut, boy, and just get an easy ride here,' but meanwhile I can hear my voice booming around the room, saying, 'No way!' Half of me is fighting this thing, but it just comes out, you know, this has to be said, and that's all there is to it. Then I'm a victim of whatever it is I've said."

"I got a big mouth—I know."

"I know a couple guys who are born liars and I admire them because it's artistry, almost. But as a means of getting along in the world, it's just destructive."

"The overblown and the pretentious—you can kill me with that shit."

"It is hard to tell people how you feel sometimes, but it's only how you feel and it's only one opinion. It doesn't have to kill him."

"How could I now possibly remember the lie I told somebody a month ago?"

—in response to a comment about his truthfulness

"When I don't know the truth."

—when asked on what occasion he lies

VIDEO

"I think there's a confusion with videos and music. You're mixing two senses. You've got the eyes, which will always take the flash, and you're trying to use them to take in the music."

"The eyes are the whores of the senses."

"I've always been suspicious of TV. I've always found music and video to be an unhappy marriage."

"MTV turned it into a money-making proposition by making people look at songs. They're selling records by eyesight, you know? You're confusing the senses. If you had a blindfold on, you can get into music ten times more effectively than watching preconceived images of what the song means."

"Why can't video find its own niche in life and get off music's back?"

THE VOICE

"To me a voice is a means of expression. And any idea about purity or technique—I mean, there's millions of great voices out there, but they chill me to death. It's a matter of whether you can touch with it, you know."

WEAVING

"There's one guy, he's just got four arms."

"The whole secret, if there is any secret behind the sound of the Rolling Stones, is the way we work two guitars together."

"The ancient form of weaving. Ronnie and I pride ourselves on people saying, 'Who played that, and who played that?' Because we figure we're playing well and nobody can tell who's doing what—that's what it's all about."

"Virtuosity is fine, but my thing has always been what two guitar players can get going together. Or three or four. If you get the right guy to play with, you can sound like an orchestra."

"On our own, we're both pretty lousy, but together we're better than ten."

—on who is a better guitar
player—he or Ronnie

WINGING IT

"When it's time to go on, it's time to go on, and when you get up there you either croak, puke, fall over, or not."

WOMEN

"Women are a beautiful complication, and I look forward to more complications."

"I like them all."

"Show me a woman who is faithful, and I won't believe you."

"There's nothing more disturbing than two chicks whispering to each other."

"If Johnson had just been a little nicer to his chicks, knew how to play the ladies a little better, then he might have been there instead of Muddy."

—on the mysterious, died-too-young
blues legend Robert Johnson

"Because we couldn't remember their fucking names."

—*explaining the choice of the title* Some Girls

"Chicks are endlessly fascinating to me. They're always an education. Women have a different point of view on things and they're not afraid to point out that I've been behaving like an asshole. And I kinda like that."

"A large percentage of American women wouldn't be half as liberated if it wasn't for the Rolling Stones."

"I've had more close calls with women than with fucking dope."

WORK

"That's the hardest work of all, bein' lazy. But you can't just make a profession out of laziness—you have to work really hard at it."

"There's this perennial thing that people have—*How do you do it?* How do you go to an office every day? Compared to that, my job is easy."

"Some people equate good work with being difficult to do, but a lot of the time it's the easiest thing. It just sort of flashes by you so quick that people virtually tell you. You didn't even see it yourself."

"I can't even spell the word."

—on retiring

"I have to work. What else would I do? Lie in bed and go mad?"

WRITING and INVENTION
(see also SONGWRITING)

"I look for ambiguity when I'm writing because life is ambiguous."

"I like ambiguity. Suggestion and insinuation is a deeper way of touching people than trying to be explicit ... I don't think rock 'n' roll is especially made for preaching."

"If I start to think about what do they want to hear, then I say I'm out of here. The only times people have liked my stuff is when I've done it because I like it."

"I don't write a diary. I'm not baring my soul. I'm trying to distill things and feelings that I've had through my life and I know for damn sure that other people have had, and I try and evoke them. You can take what's happening to you and relate to it, and it will have a totally different meaning to you than it will to somebody else."

"I don't consider that you create or write anything. The best way to think about it, for me anyway, is that you're an antenna. I sit down at an instrument—guitar, piano, bass, or whatever—and play somebody else's songs. And usually within twenty minutes, more or less, suddenly something's coming. And that's when the antenna goes up. [wets his finger and raises it in the air] Incoming! ... You work it up a bit and then transmit it."

"The idea that 'I wrote that,' or 'I created that,' is an overblown artistic sort of thing that people love to put on writing songs. It can screw you up. If you think that it's all down to you, you've got another thing coming."

"I'll get my guitar out ... play some Elvis, Buddy Holly, anything that I can remember. And after that I'll start to branch out and come up with something of my own."

"You have to let it out somewhere. There's two sides to everybody, and the shit I like to sing about is always very bittersweet. I like vulnerability but only as long as it's expressed right. 'Cause there's a thin line between vulnerable and asshole. Vulnerability has to have an edge on it ... I don't mind getting up there and say-ing, Ouch, it hurts ... If things don't hurt at all, you're numb, and that's the worst. My songs are about where to touch and when to touch ... You have to say a few things you wouldn't want to put in anybody else's mouth, and not just write something because it fits the image. Then you're just writing ads for yourself."

—on writing "Angie" and "Wild Horses"

"I receive and transmit—it's that simple. If I actually believe I created something, I'd be in big fucking trouble. There's no godhead ego, I don't believe in the grand, bold-type, WRITTEN BY KEITH RICHARDS. I just pick up the songs and pass them on. They aren't mine, they're everybody's. To me, the best songs are the ones that come to you in dreams."

"I have no idea what the audience makes of me ... Writing songs is a peculiar practice anyway. I never feel I write them, I'm just an antenna and the songs are already zooming through the room, and I hope to pick up something. I sit with a guitar or at the piano and play my favorite Buddy Holly or Otis Redding ... and, with a bit of luck, something suddenly happens and you're off on your own track."

"Sometimes we write songs in installments—just get the melody and music, and we'll cut the tracks and write the words later. That way the actual tracks have matured just like wine—you just leave it in the cellar for a bit, and it comes out a little better a few years later."

"I never wanted to do a solo record until I started doing it."

"I hate things that have only one meaning. I want words to pull triggers."

"First I find a riff and a chord sequence. And if that's any good, then I start to play it with some other guys and pump it up ... There's no point in writing songs on a sheet of paper ... I can't divorce lyrics from the music. Songwriting is a marrying of the both ... The odd brilliant and rare occasions where a song actually presents itself to you in totality from the beginning to the end ... is very rare."

"It's humbling, because you realize, Hey, I didn't write this. I just happened to be around when it came by."

"People today run themselves into a corner thinking they actually created these things. I'd rather look upon myself as an antenna or some go-between. I'm just around. Songs are running around—they're all there, ready to grab. You play an instrument and pick it up."

"I'll go through the Buddy Holly songbook ... start playing 'em for half an hour. Let's try Eddie Cochran or the Everly Brothers ... After about an hour, I get fed up with other people's songs ... theirs suggests something else to me, and I'll start to follow that. It'll either end up as a song or it'll end up as a disaster."

"I never sit down and say, 'Time to write a song. Now I'm going to write.' To me, that would be fatal ... I always like to sit down and play the guitar a couple of hours a day, and something will come ... 'Hey, there it is,' and then I hang on to the end and follow the motherfucker. The important thing is recognizing something when it comes by."

"If you can write one song, you can write nine hundred. They're there. Your method of going about that—you can either try and regiment it, make it a task, or you can make it part of your everyday life and just sit around and play and not think about writing. Play anything you want."

"I can thank Andrew Oldham for many things, but more than anything forcing me to sit down to write these horrendous songs, 'cause when you start it's always the worst. We'd farm them off to somebody else 'cause we didn't wanna know. You've gotta get all that shit outta your system before you can really start writing."

—on early Stones songs

"My favorite Keef riff? I play it all the time! Every one's the same, it's a variation on the same old thing!"

"I haven't written it yet."

—when asked what his best song is

"Nobody creates anything. It's there, and you just fucking grab a hold of it."

"It's like life. It's all a little jagged and a little misunderstood."

—referring to his songs

YOUTH

"If only the whole world could stay young."

"They don't like young kids with a lot of money. But as long as you don't bother them, that's cool. But we bothered them."

—on the press and "the establishment's" reaction to youth

"Some people have said it all by the time they're twenty-two or twenty-five, but I don't get that feeling with Hendrix or Joplin. I don't think they were finished."

"The age thing almost becomes a reverse racism. If we were Muddy Waters, nobody would talk about it. We have to deal with a twenty-five-year-old guy with a paunch sitting there, going, 'How can they do it?' You try it, brother. It keeps you in shape."

"We're happy to have the kids screaming for us. It gets me down to think that a lot of them will one day disappear into the drab mews. I hope all of them won't."

"I was just learnin' how to get busted ... researching police cells."
—on his early twenties

"Impetuous youth? Gone!"

SPECIAL BONUS SECTION: INSULTS

"I couldn't warm to him if I was cremated next to him."
on Chuck Berry

"Are you kidding me? He used to rape, loot, and pillage all over the place."
—comparing Chuck Berry to a pirate

"He's always scared of giving something for free."
—again on Chuck Berry

"He gave me more headaches than Mick Jagger."
—on Chuck Berry, once more

"I've worked with two of the toughest bitches of all time. That's why I could handle Chuck. 'You know who I've been working with for the last twenty-five years? You're chicken feed.' "

"He's a Frenchman. We can't help them."
—on Jean-Luc Godard

"He was out of his depth in England. Like William the Conqueror."
—on Jean-Luc Godard, once again

"Skyrocket to oblivion."
—on Mick Taylor

"His writing is limited to songs for dead blondes."

—on Elton John

"I absolutely draw the line at elephants. Even with trousers on. I've paid me dues. I worked with Elton and that's enough!"

"Oh man, what an old bitch."

—again, on Elton

"Reg and Rod swore they would never leave Britain. The minute their mansions were threatened they were in L.A. like a shot."

—on Elton John and Rod Stewart

"There's more to it than saying 'shit' on TV or learning how to spit by practicing in front of a mirror."

—on the Sex Pistols

"You get Duran Duran come [*sic*] down for a day, walk into our fucking sessions and say, 'What are you doing in that room together?' It's called playing music. That's the only way we record, you snotty little turd."

"People told me to listen to Beck, but that didn't take long."

"I don't know where Metallica's inspiration comes from but if it's me, then I fucked up."

"I've had enough of bloody rap. I mean, 'Mary had a little lamb, his fleece was white as fuckin' snow.' This is kindergarten shit."

"I think he'd been to too many nightclubs."

—on Mick doing "Miss You" as a disco song

"What do you do with lead vocalists? They're fairies. You've got to let them have their head and then rein them in."

—on Mick

"The only joy I got out of being a frontman was I didn't have to look at his ass."

—referring, of course, to Mick's

"Mick doesn't really like to dwell on the past. Actually, he prefers to deny it."

"If they ever find him dead, it won't be me that did it. I've already opened my mouth too much."

—on Mick

"There's no joy in punching a wimp."

—again, on Mick

"I don't want to talk to Mick about his love life, because it's like, 'Whoops! You've skidded on another banana skin!' "

"Mick's got to stop slapping paint all over his face to that absurd Japanese-theater degree. He's got to stop running around the stage and getting himself out of breath in the first ten minutes."

"Try to stay out of Mick's face as much as possible—because the more you get into Mick's face, the more makeup goes on."

—advice to Martin Scorsese

"His underpants, three times."

—responding to the question of how much Mick has changed over the years

"I don't think anything about them. Personally, I don't think he should think anything about them either."

—on Mick's solo records

"Believe me, Mick's business head is greatly exaggerated. Just leave it at that. My best weapon businesswise is a silent Mick."

"What's so *hard* about being Mick Jagger? It's like Bob Dylan's phrase: 'What's so hard about being one of the Beatles?' Although you could say that about *Bob*, you know."

"Mick Jagger's really good when he's with the Rolling Stones. But when he ain't, I don't think anybody gives a fuckin' toss."

"Somebody that's always good for an airport picture on page three."
—on Bianca Jagger

"Maybe Bill's happy running his restaurants and marrying people he never sees again. I don't know."
—on Bill Wyman

"I think he's on his third menopause, certainly can't be his first."
—again, on Bill Wyman

"I couldn't, in all honesty, get through Bill's book because I got fed up with each chapter ending up with his bank account. 'And after all that I only had five thousand pounds in the bank.'"
—on Wyman's autobiography

"Yeah—try *livin'* off of it."
—in response to "All You Need Is Love"

"I hope Ian Anderson doesn't get into a cliché thing with his leg routine."
—on Jethro Tull

"Who wants that freaky acidhead flute player teaching you about tax?"
—on Ian Anderson's comments about the Stones being tax exiles

"They're in their own little fantasy world. You only have to read what they talk about in interviews ... how many suits they've got and that kind of crap. It's all kid stuff, isn't it?"
—on the Bee Gees

"Everyone's a load of crap. They're all trying to be somebody else and they ain't being themselves. The Libertines, Arctic Monkeys, Bloc Party? Load of crap, load of crap. Poseurs, rubbish."

"They don't have the stamina to be rock stars."

—on the punks of the 1970s

"Prince is like the Monkees. A Pee-wee Herman trip. He's appealing to the same audience."

"Shave and go home. He's a wimp in disguise."

—on George Michael

"Ronnie ... drags me up and goes, 'You gotta see this chick, man.' I was already hip to it. 'Her name's George, Ron.'"

—on Boy George

"These guys are just obnoxious. Grow up and then come back and see if you can hang."

—on Oasis

"Now they're forcing Mick Ronson on people. They're lucky they got away with Bowie."

"Who's David Bowie? Oh, he went to the same art school as me."

"A Holiday Inn band, a club band that made it."

—on Gloria Estefan and Miami Sound Machine

"Nirvana? The name sounds promising. Is it a lot of blokes with long hair and guitars around their necks?"

"You're not gonna solve the problems of this world with a few rock concerts on a satellite deal and a knighthood to the guy that put it together. That's like tryin' to put a Band-Aid on a rash."

—on Live Aid

"I never understood why someone would want to have some gangster from L.A. poking his fingers in your face."

—on hip-hop

"I haven't had much of a listen to what's around at the moment. But if that MTV show is any indication, I'm not missing a lot."

"I like Bruce ... He ain't no brilliant artist ... He's holding the fort until something good comes along. If there was anything better around, he'd still be working the bars of New Jersey ... He'd be the first to say so ... But in the absence of anything better, Bruce is filling a good gap. What else you got?"

—on Bruce Springsteen

"A couple of clueless Ernies from the Midlands."

—on Robert Plant and John Bonham

"He's trying to steal my headlines."

—on Sid Vicious's suicide
while Keith was on a
drug charge in Canada

"Who are you supposed to be—Alfred Hitchcock?"

—to neophyte film director Ben Stiller

"There are certain guys that are band players and there's certain guys that ain't. If there's anybody lazier than me, it's Eric."

—on Eric Clapton

"I ain't too interested in white bands who rip off white bands who ripped off black bands."

"That he's not in it!"

—finishing a reporter's comment
that the Kinks' Ray Davies has
one problem with the Stones

"Bob's a nasty little bugger. I remember him saying to me, 'I could have written 'Satisfaction,' but you couldn't have written 'Desolation Row.' "

—on Bob Dylan

"The prophet of profit."

—again, on Bob Dylan

CHAPTER SIX

EVERYTHING
(maybe) WANTED
KEITH
BUT WERE (maybe)

YOU ALWAYS
TO KNOW ABOUT
RICHARDS
AFRAID TO ASK

NICKNAMES: Keef, The Human Riff, The World's Most Elegantly Wasted Human, and, as a child, Ricky

LIKES: Stealing ashtrays (hobby from the 1970s)
Sausages and mashed potatoes, shepherd's pie, heroin
Five sugars in tea or coffee
Canned ravioli for sauce on spaghetti
Playing dominoes
Staying up late. Or, better yet: staying up for four days straight
Hoagy Carmichael, Muddy Waters, Elvis Presley, Chuck Berry, Howlin' Wolf, Scottie Moore, Eddie Cochran, and, of course, AC/DC
Favored quality in a woman: Understanding

DISLIKES: Elton John

PHOBIA: Cheese*

IF HE COULD BE ANYTHING IN THE WORLD, HE WOULD BE: A dream

INFLUENCED: Pete Townshend's signature windmill guitar move, Johnny Depp's Jack Sparrow character in *Pirates of the Caribbean,* countless rock 'n' roll guitar players from 1964 onward, the early punk-rock aesthetic, the personal style of a few women, including Patti Smith, Chrissie Hynde, and the feminist provocateur Camille Paglia, the song "Keith Don't Go" by Nils Lofgren, and numerous lame jokes about age and death.

BIG DREAM: To write "Legless Trousers," a bio of no-legged World War II pilot Douglas Gader

PETS: A mouse in childhood—saved from a kid who threatened to kill it; several cats and dogs, mostly strays. There was one mutt named Syphilis, one named Ratbag (smuggled out of U.S. customs), some dogs rescued from Russia (including one renamed the Czar of Connecticut) and one who ate a dry food called Mick. Has long had a reputation for being kind to animals.

IMPRESSIVE ACCOMPLISHMENT: Started his own urban legend: that he went regularly to Switzerland for blood transfusions

UNIMPRESSIVE NON-ACCOMPLISHMENTS: Car crashes. Has a fondness for fancy cars, particularly Bentleys, but he may be one of the worst drivers in the Western Hemisphere. Numerous accidents, most due to speeding. Rarely drives anymore. ("They won't let me.")

HOBBY: Guitar. Owns approximately three thousand. Favors a 1950s Fender Telecaster. Tunes guitar to an open G. Often removes the lower E string. Has I'M INNOCENT inscribed on his guitar picks.

FAVORITE MOVIES: Hitchcock's *Murder*, *The Thirty-nine Steps*, *The Man Who Would Be King*.

PSEUDONYMS: Often gave himself the name Mr. Bentley when checking into hotels, but beyond this, the most typical name change was when he was asked by manager Andrew Loog Oldham to drop the *S* from Richards in the 1960s. Ten years later, in an act of protracted rebellion, he put the *S* back in.

EARLY JOBS: Many, and none glamorous: A milk route (but never being an early riser, that one ended fast), a post office gig, a ball boy at a tennis court (weekends, from ages eight to thirteen), and demonstrating refrigerators and washing machines with his mother. After earning his first twelve pounds, he yelled, "I'm rich!"

EARLY ACCOMPLISHMENTS: Won first fight by using a bicycle chain.

THE RECORDS HE'D TAKE TO A DESERT ISLAND: Chuck Berry's "Little Queenie," anything by Bach and Mozart, "Still a Fool" by Muddy Waters, Buddy Holly's "That'll Be the Day," "Mystery Train" by Elvis Presley, "Reach Out" by the Four Tops, doo-wop from the Jive Five, and some Segovia.

WHAT HE'D HAVE BEEN IF HE HADN'T JOINED THE STONES: "A layabout. But a very high-class one."

*REGARDING THE CHEESE:
Ron Wood first brought it up in 1974, saying that Keith runs screaming from rooms when he comes into contact with cheese. Keith has gone on record since then, saying it's the one thing he'll never put in his body.

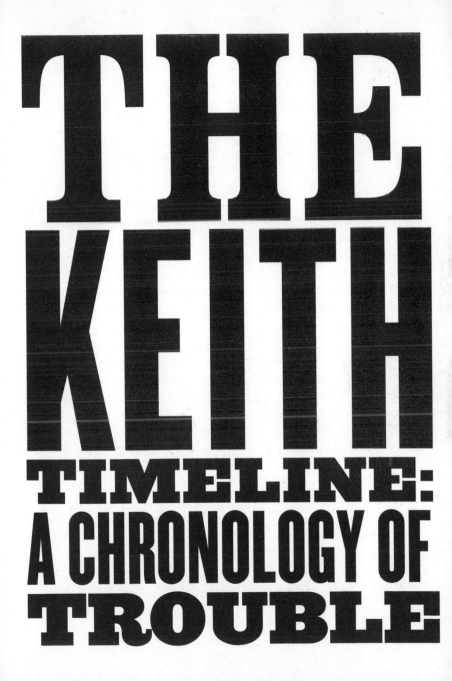

THE KEITH TIMELINE:
A CHRONOLOGY OF TROUBLE

PRE-KEITH KEITH.

Keith's family origins are in Europe's religiously violent past. His mother's father's side is from Wales, originally descended from the Huguenots — Protestants who fled Catholic France in Elizabethan times due to violent religious suppression — and settled near Canterbury. On his father's side, the roots go back to Wales as well, then onward to East London in the 1800s, where they ended up as factory laborers. His mother, Doris Dupree Richards, got pregnant with Keith to avoid factory work during World War II. His father, Bert, wasn't so lucky, and spent several years in a light-bulb factory, leaving before dawn and returning after dark, setting the stage for a miserable household. According to *Rolling Stone* magazine, the only time Bert left England up until Keith's child-hood was to go to France for the war: "And that was to get his leg blown up."

DECEMBER 18, 1943.

Keith Richards is born on a Saturday night at Livingstone Hospital in Dartford, Kent, England (which had been a stop on the pilgrims' road to Canterbury). He's born at the same hospital where Mike Jagger was delivered five months earlier to more upwardly mobile parents, as opposed to the downwardly mobile Richardses. December 18 is an auspicious birth date for someone who would develop a strong interest in both America and black culture. It's the day that the Mayflower landed at Plymouth, as well as the day the Thirteenth Amendment, which abolished slavery, was ratified.

CHILDHOOD.

By his own accounts, he grew up "in a wasteland," with bombings, war rationings, and school hazings. He is a little runt of a mama's boy, chubby, with a chronic cold and a runny nose. But he has a dream—to be Roy Rogers: "He could shoot, play the guitar, and ride a great horse. What more do you want?" Little Keith "Ricky" Richards dresses up as Rogers, with cowboy hat and holsters, but is well-known as a crybaby. A lonely only child in a working-class family, he soon finds an outlet in music, as influenced by his bandleader grandfather, Gus Dupree, who keeps a guitar lying about when Keith comes to visit (as soon as he leaves it goes back in the case). He meets Mike Jagger at around age four. (The number sometimes changes according to who is telling the story, and when.) Together they attend Wentworth County Primary School. While Mike is a good student and outgoing, Keith is neither. Still, a teacher comments that Keith is "a straightforward type of person. He laughs when he is happy, cries when he is sad. There is no problem in trying to find out what is going on inside his mind. He's open, frank." But despite her kind words, it's not easy. He cries all morning and needs to be forced to school. It's the beginning of a long, bad relationship: School and Keith go together like oil and water.

1951 or 1953 (accounts vary) – Along with the two other biggest hoods in school, Spike and Terry, he becomes a choir boy. It was a good way to get out of science class.

They are three bad boys with the sweetest voices and tight jeans under their surplices. Their highlight comes in singing for the queen at Westminster Abbey, 1953 (although skeptics wonder if Keith made that up). "All my gigs have gone right downhill since."

1954 (accounts vary) – Joins the Boy Scouts as part of the "Beaver Patrol" but quits six months later, not liking being told what to do.

1955 – A move to the wrong side of the tracks.

The Richardses move to Spielman Road—government housing

for the working class, i.e., the projects. It is, by his account, "Soul-destroying. A disgusting concrete jungle of horrible new streets full of rows of semidetached houses." Plus, he's regularly beaten up.

1956 – His voice breaks, and he's kicked out of the choir.
It's his first taste of the heartlessness of show business. He doesn't take it well. Keith quickly becomes a more impressively bad student. It is noted on the sidelines, however, that he has a talent for drawing.

1956 – With increasingly poor grades at school, Keith is sent to Dartford Technical College, "where underachievers learn manual trades."
Resentful over being kicked out of the chorus, and beefing up his defiance of authority, he messes up more, is made to repeat a year, then tops it off by getting expelled. Neighbors plan on seeing him in the gutter in the future. The guitar playing at Grandpa's, however, continues to go well.

1958 – Age fifteen. Gets his first guitar for his birthday. Soon after, his first record player.
The guitar is a Rosetti acoustic, which his mother buys for about seven pounds with money earned from her job at a bakery. He practices repeatedly from a spot at the top of the stairs. Grandpa starts him off by teaching him "Malaguena." He develops a fascination with America and its music, and teaches himself Elvis's "That's All Right, Mama" and "Blue Moon of Kentucky." The first record he buys is a Woolworth imitation of a Ricky Nelson song. Listens to all new artists from America, including Little Richard and Jerry Lee Lewis.

1959 or 1960 (accounts on year vary) – Thrown out of Dartford Tech for "insolence," poor attendance, and questionable fashion style; he's sent to Sidcup Art College,
so unimpressive a school that it is eventually demolished and replaced by a supermarket. It's a "last chance" for students headed nowhere, simi-

lar to Hope Street in Liverpool, where John Lennon was sent in 1958. Other art-school losers from 1959–1962: Pete Townshend, Ray Davies, Jimmy Page, David Bowie, and Ron Wood. During this time Keith meets Dick Taylor—who will become one of the original Rolling Stones.

1959 – Discovers Chuck Berry
and realizes music is what he wants to devote his life to. He develops a troubled relationship with his father. Within a year, the two stop speaking almost entirely.

1960 – Performs for the first time in public, at a sports dance at Eltham.
Most of the audience has walked out before he gets to finish. After the show, he misses the last train home and spends the night freezing at a bus shelter.

October 1961 (accounts vary: some say 1960) – Keith meets soon-to-be evil twin Mike Jagger on train to London.
It's the first time Keith has seen Mike since he bought an ice cream off of him a few years earlier. What really interests him are the records Mike is carrying—rare American imports, including Chuck Berry and Muddy Waters. "Just sitting in that train carriage in Dartford, it was almost like we made a deal without knowing it, like Robert Johnson at the crossroads. There was a *band* made there, that despite everything else, goes on and on. Like a solid deal." Keith invites Mike over to his house, they begin hanging out more, and then Mike invites Keith to join his band, Little Boy Blue and the Blue Boys.

April 7, 1962 – Keith and Mike/Mick meet Brian Jones (aka Elmo Lewis).
Jones is the *real* bad boy—complete with a posse of illegitimate children and a rotation of jobs he's been fired from for stealing.

May 1962 – Brian Jones advertises for bandmates.
First one to answer ad is Ian Stewart, a shipping clerk at a chemical factory.

June 1962 – Keith and Mick join Brian Jones's band.
Their aim is to become the greatest blues band in England.

July 12, 1962 – Brian names the band the Rollin' Stones.
They debut at the Marquee in London. Other members include bassist Dick Taylor—the friend of Keith's from Sidcup—and drummer Mike Avery.

August 1962 – Keith moves in with Mick and Brian at 102 Edith Grove,
a filthy flat with barely any heat. They live at near-starvation level, and take turns stealing food and money-back bottles from parties.

September 1962 – Dick Taylor quits, losing faith in the band's ability to have any success, and decides to devote himself to the more level-headed pursuit of art school.

October 1962 – Keith's parents separate and divorce.

December 1962 – Bill Wyman, aka Bill Perks, joins the band.
Older than the others (but presented to the public with a false younger age), he comes from a childhood of poverty and is the only one with the shockingly square credentials of marriage and military service. However, he has some great amplifiers.

January 1963 – Band changes name to the Rolling Stones from the Rollin' Stones.

January 1963 – Charlie Watts joins as drummer.
He is working as a graphic artist and still living with his parents. When the band members insist that he signs on, his response is, "Yeah, all right then, but I don't know what my dad's gonna say." He imagines the stint will last about a year.

January 14, 1963 – First Stones gig in Soho, at the Flamingo.

February 24, 1963 – First gig at the Crawdaddy Club, London. They soon become the house band.

April 1963 – First write-up on the band: a thumbs-up from the *Richmond and Twickenham Times*.

April 14, 1963 – Beatles come to the club to see the Stones play.

April 24, 1963 – The Stones are turned down by the BBC.

April 28, 1963 – Andrew Loog Oldham, an assistant to the Beatles' Brian Epstein, sees the Stones perform.
His tycoon antenna goes up, and days later he signs an exclusive deal for management. Ian Stewart is taken out of the lineup about three days later for being too square, and is given what will become a lifelong job as road manager and occasional pianist. Oldham sets to work pumping up the bad-boy image. A typical concoction fed to the press, one that Keith doesn't much care for: The Stones don't wash or change clothes for a week.

May 1963 – Decca signs the Stones and they record their first single the next day.
The executive who signs them is Dick Rowe, who infamously turned down the Beatles. George Harrison suggested he rectify his mistake by going to see the Stones.

June 7, 1963 – Decca releases the first Stones single, "Come On"/ "I Wanna Be Loved."

July 1963 – First TV appearance, on *Thank Your Lucky Stars*.
Among the letters to the TV station: "I have seen today the most disgusting sight I can remember in all my years as a television fan."

July 1963 – The official Rolling Stones fan club now has three hundred members.

September 1963 – John Lennon and Paul McCartney write "I Wanna Be Your Man" for the Stones.

September 1963 – Keith moves with Mick into new apartment
at 33 Mapelsbury Road, London, at nine pounds a week. "We can get together there on songwriting in the sort of atmosphere that suits us best. It's chaos, but our sort of chaos."

September 29, 1963 – First major Stones tour beings, with Bo Diddley and the Everly Brothers.

November 1963 – "I Wanna Be Your Man" reaches number nine on U.K. chart.

December 1963 – The Stones do soundtracks for Rice Krispies commercials.

January 1964 – The Stones tour as headline act with the Ronettes.

January 24, 1964 – Debut U.K. album *The Rolling Stones* becomes instant hit.
Opens with "Not Fade Away" and includes "Route 66." Debuts in the U.S. two months later.

March 1964 – Marianne Faithfull enters the picture.
She's a "convent girl" whom they meet at a party. She eventually sleeps with Brian, Keith, and Mick, and settles on bachelor number three. Years later, she claims Keith provided "the best night of [her] life." She brings a literary influence to the band's songs and glamour to their image. Plus a good deal of trouble.

1964 – Model Linda Keith is "arranged" by Oldham to be Keith's first swank public girlfriend.

"I thought it was time that Keith went out with something other than his guitar," notes Oldham. She lives the Keith Richards life before he does. The relationship lasts several years, until Keith calls her parents and tells on her for overuse of drugs. She is later confined to a psychiatric hospital.

June 1, 1964 – The Stones arrive in the U.S. for first American tour. Keith is twenty years old.

June 3, 1964 – *The Hollywood Palace* TV show. Dean Martin famously insults the Stones.

1964 – While in Chicago, Keith reportedly sees hero Muddy Waters painting the ceiling at Chess Records.

July 4, 1964 – Appearance on *Juke Box Jury*.

A reviewer for *The Daily Sketch* comments: "A group of Neanderthal young men who call themselves the Rolling Stones sat in judgment as the jury men. It was a mockery of a trial."

July 24, 1964 – Blackpool, Scotland: Keith kicks audience member in head.

Rowdy hoods spit at Brian, and Keith warns them to back off. They then spit on Keith. He retaliates by stepping on their knuckles and kicking one guy square in the nose. An anti-Stones riot ensues, and Keith is nearly killed.

July 31–August 1, 1964 – Another riot: Belfast.

August 8, 1964 – Another riot: Holland.

September 1964 – "As Tears Go By," first original song by Jagger and Richards, makes top ten.

It comes to the public via a recording by Faithfull, written after

Oldham locked Mick and Keith in a room together and wouldn't let them out until they had something finished.

September 1964 – Apartment is robbed and ransacked while the Stones are on tour.

October 13, 1964 – *12 × 5* is released,
includes "Time Is On My Side" and "Good Times, Bad Times."

October 25, 1964 – *Ed Sullivan Show*.
"To him, we were just some drag act. All that stuff, it was like you were just thrown in the deep end … 'You're on after the elephants!' At that time we must have been the most bizarre thing he'd ever seen. The elephants were normal to him."

1965 – The Stones officially become an international phenomenon.
They meet Allen Klein, the supermanager who would get them the world's greatest record deal, but also screw them out of millions.

February 1965 – Audiences get more hysterical, including instances of the "suicide wish," in which girls jump off of the balconies.

February 13, 1965 – *The Rolling Stones, Now!* is released.
Songs include "Heart of Stone" and "Little Red Rooster."

February 1965 – Keith tells *Melody Maker*: "I'll probably die of an electric shock."

March 18, 1965 – The Stones arrested for urinating on wall
after being refused bathroom in East London. Rationale: "We'll piss anywhere, man."

May 2, 1965 – *Ed Sullivan Show* once more, even though Ed claimed he wouldn't do it again:
"I received hundreds of letters from parents complaining about you."

May 6, 1965 – Keith writes "Satisfaction" in his sleep
at Fort Harrison Hotel in Clearwater, Florida, after a concert at Jack Russell Stadium: "I woke up in the middle of the night. There was a cassette player next to the bed and an acoustic guitar. I pushed 'record' and hit that riff for about a minute and a half ... Then I fell back to sleep." When he replayed it the next day, "It was two minutes of 'Satisfaction' and forty minutes of me snoring." It almost got scrapped (Keith thought it sounded like filler), then became the band's first number-one hit. *Newsweek* called the riff "five notes that shook the world." The hotel is now a Scientology church.

June 1965 – Keith is technically "homeless," living at the Hilton Hotel. It's the start of a high-end nomadic existence.

September 11–17, 1965 – Berlin: more riots.

September 13–14, 1965 – More dangerous than a riot: Anita Pallenberg enters the story.
At a concert in Munich, the Italian-German model with the "diamond grin" makes her way backstage, charms Brian Jones, and immediately moves in on Stones territory as his girlfriend. She has a strong influence on Brian and, later, Keith. Sometimes called the Sixth Stone (the same honor given to Ian Stewart), her interests are in black magic and pushing buttons. Rumored to be a witch, she is one tough girl: "Brian tried to beat Anita up and broke his ribs in the process."

October 3, 1965 – Knocked unconscious onstage from "flying debris"
in Manchester. Whether it was falling from above the stage or flung from the audience is debated.

December 3, 1965 – Electrocuted onstage but saved by Hush Puppies.

During the song "The Last Time," Keith falls unconscious in Sacramento. He lives thanks to his rubber-soled Hush Puppies. "I woke up an hour later ... with a doctor saying, 'They either come around or they don't.' " It is a bizarre prediction come to fruition after his comment to *Melody Maker* ten months earlier.

December 4, 1965 – *December's Children* is released.

Includes "As Tears Go By" and "Get Off My Cloud."

1966 – Separates from Linda Keith.

Reportedly leaves phone messages for years that say, "Tell Linda to fuck off." "Ruby Tuesday" is generally believed to be his swan song to Linda.

1966 – Düsseldorf: Police hose thousands of fans as mob breaks past security.

March 29, 1966 – Paris: Near-riot.

Police take eighty-five fans into custody.

March–April 1966 – Riot: Marseilles.

Overly enthusiastic fan throws chair at stage, nearly blinding evil twin.

May 1966 – Keith purchases Redlands in Sussex, England, a mansion with a moat that will soon bring him significant trouble.

June 2, 1966 – *Aftermath*, the band's first album of all-original material, is released,

includes "Paint It Black" and "Under My Thumb."

July 2, 1966 – Riot and tear gas: Forest Hills, New York.

Sept 11, 1966 – *Ed Sullivan Show* again.
Brian falls down in Morocco, breaks his hand, and almost blows it for them.

October 1966 – Moves in with Brian and Anita at 1 Courtfield Road, London.

January 13, 1967 – More near-death fiascos.
Stones arrive in New York for *Ed Sullivan Show*. At the airport, the limo is nearly run over by a taxiing jet. Then, denied access at the Sullivan Theatre, Keith punches doorman out and dumps a bucket of garbage over his head.

January 20, 1967 – *Between the Buttons* is released.
Songs include "Ruby Tuesday" and "Let's Spend the Night Together."

February 12, 1967 – Police raid a party at Redlands, Keith's home in Sussex, England.
Dylan's "Visions of Johanna" is playing on the record player as arrest is made. The words "the ghost of electricity" blast out and the subject of electrocution haunts Keith once again.

February 25–March 16, 1967 – Keith changes the backdrop.
Goes to Morocco with Brian, Mick, Marianne, and Brian's girlfriend, Anita. It ends with Keith taking off with Anita and leaving Brian stranded in Tangier. There's two ways to look at the story: Either Keith was a knight in shining armor who saved Anita as Brian beat her up, or it was the ultimate act of betrayal. "A lot can go on in the backseat of a Bentley. What can anyone say? Shit happens."

March 27, 1967 – Sweden: riot.
Chairs, bottles, fireworks, and thrown stones.

April 14, 1967 – Zurich: Near-riot.

April 1967 – Vienna: Riot.

Smoke bomb. One hundred and fifty fans are arrested.

May 10, 1967 – Keith pleads not guilty to offenses from Redlands bust.

Huge crowd arrives to cheer and hiss.

June 27–29, 1967 – The drug trial lasts for days and ends with the unwanted verdict: guilty.

June 29, 1967 – Enters Wormwood Scrubs Prison.

He's deloused, given number 7855 and a blunt spoon to eat with, and prepares to spend a year sewing mailbags. He writes to Mum and says, "Don't worry." The ruling is reversed, and he's out the next day.

July 17, 1967 – *Flowers* is released.

Cover shows each band member as a flower on a stem. There are no leaves on Brian's stem. Songs include "Ruby Tuesday," "Let's Spend the Night Together," and "Mother's Little Helper."

Summer 1967 – The transformation and makeover of Keith.

He spends summer in Rome as Anita works on the film *Barbarella*. In her role as the Dark Queen, she makes costar Jane Fonda look like Howdy Doody. Keith starts wearing Anita's clothes, jewels, and makeup. Gets trademark shag hairdo. The new, improved Keith "look" starts to take shape.

November 15, 1967 – *Their Satanic Majesty's Request* is released.

The Stones version of *Sgt. Pepper* includes the tracks "2,000 Light Years from Home" and "She's a Rainbow."

December 22, 1967 – Goes to Tangier with Anita.

The Keith Richards look gets even more defined.

May 6, 1968 – Meets Gram Parsons,
an American Southern rock and country music artist who will become the main influence on Keith personally and musically.

June 1968 – *One Plus One* is filmed with director Jean-Luc Godard.
The genesis and development of "Sympathy for the Devil" is documented. It's also a document of Brian's physical and mental deterioration.

August 1968 – "Street Fighting Man" is released.
Purported to be about Keith's tough life growing up, it is banned from several Chicago radio stations in fear that it will incite violence during the National Democratic Convention in September.

September 1968 – Filming of *Performance*.
Warner Bros. casts Jagger in the starring role as a hermit has-been rock star, widely believed to be a composite of Brian and Keith. Anita plays his love interest, and rumors spark of a real on-set affair between the two. Keith watches trouble from the back of a limo. Actor James Fox reportedly is unhinged by on-set mind games of Jagger and Pallenberg, and has a nervous breakdown.

December 1, 1968 – *Beggars Banquet* is released,
includes "Sympathy for the Devil" and the Joan-Baez-could-have-sung-it "Salt of the Earth."

December 10–12, 1968 – *Rock 'n' Roll Circus* performance.
Three days of staying awake, taking drugs, and performing a TV concert that never airs. Brian almost doesn't show because "the Stones are being mean to me." It is Brian's last performance with the Stones. Keith performs with the Dirty Mac, a band that includes John Lennon, Yoko Ono, Eric Clapton, and Mitch Mitchell. The show is finally screened at the New York Film Festival nearly twenty-eight years later.

December 18, 1968 – Travels to Brazil, tells the press he's looking for "a certain magician."

"We've become very interested in magic and we're very serious about this trip. We hope to see this magician who practices both white magic and black magic. He has a long and difficult name, which we cannot pronounce. We call him 'Banana' for short."

1969 – Tensions rise between Keith, Mick, and Anita; heroin use intensifies.

Keith works on ideas for "Honky Tonk Women" (inspired by Gram Parsons, who some think actually wrote it), "Gimme Shelter," and "Let It Bleed."

June 7, 1969 – First car crash in a series of many.

Anita breaks collarbone while pregnant.

June 8, 1969 – Brian Jones is fired.

Keith, Mick, and Charlie drive down to Pooh Corner (aka Brian's house, the former A. A. Milne estate) and tell Brian it's over.

June 13, 1969 – Mick Taylor joins Stones.

Richards and Taylor are now seen as rock's greatest guitar duo, with Taylor's main contribution being complex extended instrumentals.

July 2, 1969 – Brian Jones dies.

He meets his end in the swimming pool at Pooh Corner. It's a nasty end, filled with speculation of suicide, murder, drugs, and a wayward asthma inhaler. Rumors persist that Keith knocked him off. With Brian gone, Keith essentially takes over where Brian left off—taking on the job of excessive, self-destructive, on-the-edge rock star.

July 4, 1969 – Two days after Brian's death, with unintentional irony, "You Can't Always Get What You Want" is released.

July 5, 1969 – Free concert in Hyde Park as memorial to Brian.

Thousands of butterflies are released in tribute, most of them already dead. The trouble develops further when it's learned that some species were illegally let go.

July 10, 1969 – Funeral for Brian.

Mobs line the street in Cheltenham. Mick and Keith are no-shows. Not a good move when there's a potentially vengeful ghost. A few days later, Brian's ghost starts trouble. Marianne Faithfull sees his ghost in a mirror in Australia, overdoses, and goes into coma.

Summer 1969 – Peruvian earring.

Keith gets his car pierced by some members of the Living Theater. He wears a heavy bone earring from Peru—exemplifying a "pick up and carry it on through life" fashion philosophy that will later extend to the tchotchkes in his hair.

Summer 1969 – Moves to 3 Cheyne Walk in Chelsea, London,

just down the street from Mick and Marianne. The former residence of a Tory minister is refashioned with a psychedelic piano and tripping room. It won't be long before it becomes another focal point of trouble.

August 10, 1969 – Keith's son Marlon is born, and now Keith has a personal child roadie.

Marlon will soon be responsible for waking Dad for concerts and snarling "Fuck off" to suspicious adults, something he becomes adept at in his first seven years. His first words are reportedly "room service."

October 1969 – Goes to L.A., takes up with Gram Parsons.

November 28, 1969 – *Let It Bleed* is released,

includes "Gimme Shelter" and "Midnight Rambler."

December 6, 1969 – Altamont: The Era of Good Feeling officially ends.

The free concert is modeled on Woodstock but turns out to be the anti-Woodstock. Along with the Manson murders, it's seen as the event that ends the "bullshit flower power" of the 1960s. There are four deaths at the concert: one murder, two automobile hit-and-runs, and one drowning. The wave of homicidal tension starts as the Stones play "Sympathy for the Devil," inciting violence that escalates into the stabbing of eighteen-year-old Meredith Hunter during "Under My Thumb." Keith: "It was just another gig where I had to leave fast."

May 26, 1970 – Charged with assault after altercation with an Italian tourist near Beaulieu-sur-Mer.

1970 – *Gimme Shelter* premieres in Cannes.

The film that documents the death and violence at Altamont gets celebrity and red-carpet treatment at Cannes. Keith and Anita attend.

July 1970 – Recording contract with Decca ends.

Told that they owe the company another single, the Stones write the pornographic "Cocksucker Blues," which has no hope of release.

July 30, 1970 – Supermanager Allen Klein is dismissed.

The guy wasn't as trustworthy as hoped.

August 1970 – *Performance* is released.

"The most disgusting, the most completely worthless film I have seen since I began reviewing."—Richard Schickel, *Time* magazine

September 4, 1970 – *Get Yer Ya-Yas Out* (live album) is released.

March 14, 1971 – The Goodbye Britain tour.

With tax problems and pressures from the government, it's time to get out. Say goodbye first.

End of March–April 6, 1971 – The Stones leave England, deemed tax exiles.

Claiming to be broke, they move to the south of France, an area W. Somerset Maugham called "a sunny place for shady people." The house Keith chooses as his home, Nellcote, is a former Gestapo headquarters. Eight months later, Keith will pull an Errol Flynn and escape from France when it proves to be too much trouble.

April 6, 1971 – The Stones sign new record deal with Atlantic Records through Kinney National, an American parking-lot corporation; Rolling Stones Records is formed.

It's at least an illusion of independence. Marshall Chess, who once answered the letters from kids in England asking for blues albums, is made president. In time, Keith will help Marshall become a heroin addict.

April 23, 1971 – *Sticky Fingers* is released.

Includes "Brown Sugar," "Wild Horses," and "Sister Morphine." While recording, the band operates according to "Keith Richards time" —he's now missing sessions, too stoned to appear.

May 14, 1971 – Mick marries himself,

aka Bianca de Macías, who has a suspiciously Micklike appearance. At the wedding, Keith reportedly passes out behind a sofa and hurls an ashtray through a window at the altar. "I think Bianca has had a bigger negative influence on Mick than anyone would have thought possible."

August 1971 – The Stones file suit against Andrew Loog Oldham

and his associate Eric Easton on charges of fraud, withheld royalties, secret agreements with Decca, and coercion. In another action, they bring suit against Allen Klein.

October 1, 1971 – Guitar collection is stolen in France.

January 1972 – Thrown off stage by Chuck Berry at the Hollywood Palladium, Los Angeles.

April 17, 1972 – Keith's daughter Dandelion is born. (Name later changed to Angela.)

May 13, 1972 – *Exile on Main Street* is released.
A double album that combines blues, country, soul, and rock. Considered the most Keith of all Stones albums, it includes his trademark song "Happy." (The source of his happiness has been debated—some say it was hearing Anita was pregnant; Keith says it was finally showing up for a session on time.) There's a strong influence from Gram Parsons on the album, as well as from Little Richard, Hank Williams, Southern spirituals, country-western, and Robert Johnson.

July 18, 1972 – Arrested in Warwick, Rhode Island, with other Stones, for assault and obstructing police due to scuffle at the airport. Keith also punches out a photographer.

July 1972 – Tour truck is destroyed by a bomb in Montreal.

August 1972 – Keith moves family to Villars, Switzerland; tries a Swiss family life and skiing.

December 1972 – Warrants are issued for the arrests of Keith and Anita in Nice, France.
The case ultimately collapses when it's revealed that police were coerced into concocting stories.

December 1972 – Keith buys his estate, Point of View, in Jamaica.

1973 – Death of grandfather Gus Dupree, the man who introduced him to music and the guitar.

1973 – Rumors start circulating that some guitarist named Ron Wood is going to replace Keith if he doesn't clean up his act.

1973 – Walking-death look gets thumbs-up.
Lester Bangs writes in *Creem* magazine: "Keith was obviously one of those people who look the absolute best of their entire lives when they're clearly on the verge of death. It seemed to lend him a whole new profundity and eloquence ... soul flattened, skin sallow, bone scraped, and behind the reflector-shaded eyes the suggestion of a diseased intelligence ... Fucked up. It was beautiful."

June 26, 1973 Police storm and ransack house at Cheyne Walk while Keith and Anita are in bed.
Found: cannabis, Mandrax, cocaine, Chinese heroin, guns, and 110 rounds of ammunition. Bail: one thousand pounds.

June 27, 1973 – Court again, for narcotics and firearms charges.
Keith and Anita are released on bail and go to Sussex, where, four days later, there's more trouble ...

July 31–August 1, 1973 – Redlands, Keith's home in Sussex, mysteriously bursts into flames.

August 1973 – Spain bans all Rolling Stones records.

August 31, 1973 – *Goats Head Soup* is released.
Contains the Keith drug song "Coming Down Again" and "Angie," which may be about Anita ("Anita-I-need-ya") or his just-born daughter Dandelion (later renamed Angela).

September 19, 1973 – Gram Parsons dies at age twenty-six from heroin overdose at a hotel room in the California desert.
The body is stolen from the Los Angeles airport, driven back to the desert, and set on fire in a Three Stooges–level amateur cremation.

The death is a major blow to Keith. From here on in, many claim to hear the ghost of Parsons in Keith's songs.

October 15, 1973 – Suspended prison sentence given by a Nice court. Keith and Anita are ordered to pay £500 each, plus an additional £205 for Keith, for possession of drugs, firearms, and ammunition. Thrilled, they throw a party at a London hotel and accidentally set the bed and the room on fire.

October 24, 1973 – Marlborough Street Court fines Keith and gives Anita a one-year discharge for the Cheyne Walk raid.

February 1974 – Keith and Anita are banned from entering France.

July 1974 – British magazine *New Music Express* calls Richards "The world's most elegantly wasted human being," an honor that will last decades.

August 1974 – Rumor starts that Richards has undergone a complete blood transfusion in Switzerland. It's later revealed the rumor was started by Keith himself.

October 18, 1974 – *It's Only Rock 'n' Roll* is released. Songs include "If You Can't Rock Me" and "Fingerprint File," purportedly about the FBI's tracking of Keith and Mick.

October 1974 – Recording of Keith's song "Scarlet" with Jimmy Page and Ian Stewart. The song is never released.

November/December 1974 – Mick Taylor quits the Stones, claiming later he had to save his life. We're not all that strong, after all.

April 14, 1975 – Ron Wood is named as newest Stone.

Dubbed "the professional second banana" and "the Henry Kissinger of the Stones," he keeps peace between Keith and Mick. He also has a Keith Jr. talent for attracting disaster.

July 5, 1975 – Keith is arrested with Keith Jr., aka newly minted partner-in-trouble Ron Wood, on Arkansas highway.

Charges: speeding and possession of an offensive weapon. The weapon: a tin-can opener. Thirty-one years later Governor Mike Huckabee will pardon him. The confiscated knife is framed and hung on wall in Arkansas courtroom.

March 26, 1976   Keith's son Tara Jo Jo Gunne Richards is born in Geneva.

April 1976 – Crashes Bentley in Buckinghamshire.

Drugs are found in wreckage and Keith is carted off once again. Rumor has it he was set up as an unwitting courier.

April 20, 1076 – *Black and Blue* is released.

Songs include "Fool to Cry" and "Memory Motel." Ron Wood makes album debut as a Stone.

May 19, 1976 – Arrested again: Newport Pagnell.

Car crash, asleep at the wheel, unidentified substance found in car.

May 1976 – Reportedly nods out onstage during concert at Earls Court, England.

June 1976 – Ten-week-old Tara dies of mysterious illness.

Keith hears the news while on tour in Paris and continues on with the show. Keith and Anita are described as a broken F. Scott and Zelda Fitzgerald. Soon after, daughter Dandelion is sent to live with Keith's mother and is raised as Keith was.

August–October 1976 – Court: Newport Pagnell.

Cocaine-possession charge. The trial spans months. Keith arrives two hours late because, he says, he was waiting for his pants to come out of the dryer. The judge: "It strikes me as extraordinary that any gentleman of this stature can only afford one pair of trousers." Pays bail.

January 10–12, 1977 – Court again.

Two counts of narcotics possession from car accident in May. It's argued a fan placed drugs in the car without Keith's knowledge. Verdict: guilty. £750 fine, plus £250 in costs, and a warning that next time he has a run-in with the police, there will be jail time.

February 1977 – Another run-in. Keith is fined £25 for driving without proper papers.

February 24, 1977 – The Toronto headache begins.

All the other brushes with the law are child's play. This time it's big. On a flight to Toronto, Keith shoots up in the bathroom and drops spoon in toilet. The spoon does him in; it leads the police to search further. They find what they're looking for. On landing at the airport, the focus turns to Anita for possession. But there's more to come. Some say Keith is framed by a disgruntled Stones insider.

February 27, 1977 – Arrest: Canadian drug police arrive at Suite 2223 at the Harbour Castle Hotel, Toronto.

It takes about forty-five minutes to wake Keith up to tell him he's under arrest. "It's pretty frightening waking up with cops all around your bed."

March 4, 1977 – Amid all the trial drama, the Stones and Keith play the first of the El Mocambo Club concerts.

To add to the drama, Margaret Trudeau, wife of the Canadian prime minister, shows up. Thanks, Margaret.

March 7–14, 1977 – On trial in Toronto.

Fans arrive en masse with "Free Keith" T-shirts, but the I-Hate-Keith contingent arrives too. One woman grabs his hair, spits at him. He is rearrested after his first day in court. Keith's attorney will go on to compare him to Billie Holiday, F. Scott Fitzgerald, Vincent Van Gogh, and Dylan Thomas, saying, "I ask your honor to understand him as a creative tortured person—as a major contributor to art. He turned to heroin to prop up a sagging existence ... He has fought a tremendous personal battle to rid himself of this terrible problem." When the judge later claims Richards's songs glorify drugs, Keith responds: "This is a misconception. I mean, about one percent of our songs glorify the use of drugs, and Mick Jagger wrote them anyway, not me."

March 1977 – "Life imprisonment at the Harbour Castle Hotel for a month."

Aka: Stranded in Canada. He records, with Ian Stewart, five despair-filled country songs he'd learned from Gram Parsons, including one about a man facing the electric chair. While at the hotel, Keith and Anita watch *Taxi Driver* repeatedly on pay TV. Anita complains that being on the high floor is like "living in an airplane." Seven-year-old Marlon acts as bodyguard, dutifully telling all meddling adults, including Margaret Trudeau, to fuck off.

April 1977 – The United States grants Keith a health visa to clean up.

He undergoes "black box" treatment for heroin in Pennsylvania, an "electro-acupuncture" process that Eric Clapton had used. While treated, Keith reportedly stays at the same house where the film *The Blob* was filmed.

June and July 1977 – Keith misses his court appearance in Toronto due to drug treatment.

September 1977 – Newport Pagnell court hearing: Bail is set at £5,000.

September 23, 1977 – *Love You Live*, recorded at the El Mocambo Club, is released.

October 1977 – The Stones come to Paris to record; Keith can't find the apartment he'd bought in 1968.

December 1977 – Keith makes it to court in Toronto at last.

February 15, 1978 – The arresting and chief investigating officer in the Toronto bust is killed in a car crash.

(Is Anita really a witch?)

June 9, 1978 – *Some Girls* is released to more headaches.

Songs include the autobiographical "Before They Make Me Run," about Toronto. Jesse Jackson launches campaign to ban the album for sexually explicit lyrics about black women. Keith responds: "We write our songs from personal experiences. Okay, so over the last fifteen years we've happened to meet extra-horny black chicks— well, I'm sorry, but I don't think I'm wrong and neither does Mick." He later expounds on the choice of the album name: "Because we couldn't remember all their fucking names."

July 1978 – Riot: Orchard Beach, New York, when Stones refuse to do encore.

September 1978 – Yet another Keith house goes up in flames

(a rental in Hollywood). "I open the door to the bedroom and I'm looking at a fireball rushing down the corridor towards the oxygen ... and me! There's the two of us stark naked. Half the house is already destroyed, the roof is falling in on us, but we've managed to get through ... to the swimming pool ... Stark fucking bullock naked with this blonde saying to me, 'Do something.' And I said, 'What do you want me to do? Piss on it?' Suddenly this car stops and it's Anita's cousin. And she goes, 'Get in!' And she just scooped us up and whisked me off so nobody could find me for a couple of days."

October 7, 1978 – Too stoned to deliver one line in a skit about drugs on *Saturday Night Live.*

October 23–24, 1978 – Crown prosecutor appeals sentence in Canada, and Keith goes back to court.
"It's Canada versus the Rolling Stones. I mean, I didn't screw Margaret Trudeau. I have to pay for the rape of Canada." Eventually, blind Toronto teenager privately appeals to the judge, citing Keith's kindness to her and his looking out for her at concerts. Through this intervention by the "Blind Angel," an order is given to perform a free concert at the Canadian Institute for the Blind.

January 1979 – Trouble with evil twin heats up.
Stones begin work on *Emotional Rescue.* The rift between Keith and Mick gets ugly. Largely because Keith is no longer "gone" in a heroin blur, when the band's operation was left to Mick.

February 1979 – Longtime Stones road manager goes missing in Bermuda Triangle. The Stones eventually find him.

April 1979 – Live concert to aid the Canadian Institute for the Blind,
as set in motion by the Blind Angel. The Stones perform with Ron Wood's band, the New Barbarians.

June 27, 1979 – Toronto court again.
Keith's statement: "I can truthfully say that the prospect of ever using drugs again in the future is totally alien to my thinking." Drug-trafficking charges are dropped.

June–July 1979 – Keith's drug dealer tells all.
Up and Down with the Rolling Stones, Tony Sanchez's lurid "memoir" about life as Keith's drug dealer, is published and serialized in the *New York Post* while the court is considering appeal.

July 20, 1979 – Seventeen-year-old shoots himself at Keith's South Salem, New York, home.

Keith isn't there, but Anita is. There are rumors of Russian roulette, teen sex orgies, drugs, and Anita being in bed with the boy when it happens. For weeks afterward, the tabloids swarm with stories about Anita's forays into black magic and the house being New York State's witch headquarters. It's the final nail in the Keith-and-Anita coffin. Separation is imminent.

December 1979 – Release of Keith's Christmas album, *Run Rudolph Run*.

December 1979 – Keith meets image-of-health fashion model Patti Hansen at his birthday party.

1980s – The Brenda Years and World War III.

Keith comes across a book by an author named Brenda Jagger at a Paris bookstore near the very same apartment he couldn't find a few years earlier. He now refers to Mick as "Brenda." Tensions between Keith and newly named Brenda get worse. Keith claims he's gearing up to replace Brenda with Roger Daltrey.

June 23, 1980 – *Emotional Rescue* is released,

includes "All About You," a Keith track about either Brenda or Anita.

July 1980 – Separation from Anita Pallenberg.

January 1981 – Eviction from New York apartment.

Keith is turned in by neighbors for loud music, specifically Hoagy Carmichael, in the early morning.

June 1981 – Goes backstage in New York City to greet his hero, Chuck Berry, who punches him and gives him a black eye.

August 30, 1981 – *Tattoo You* **is released.**
Songs include "Neighbors" (about his eviction) and "Start Me Up."

November 1981 – Performs with Muddy Waters onstage in Chicago along with Ron and Mick.

1982 – Reconciles with his father after two decades without contact.

June 1, 1982 – *Still Life* **(live album) is released.**

September 1, 1982 – Yet another major fire at the Redlands house.

1983 – Chuck Berry reportedly drops a lit match down Keith's shirt at LAX airport.
"Every time him and me got in contact, whether it's intentional or not, I end up wounded."

November 7, 1983 – *Undercover* **is released,**
includes Keith track "Wanna Hold You."

December 18, 1983 – Marries Patti Hansen on his fortieth birthday.
The fashion model from a religious Staten Island family is credited with helping get Keith off heroin. Says he is "not going to let this bitch go." He sticks to his word.

1985 – Moves to Connecticut.

1985 – "Silver and Gold" recorded with U2.

March 18, 1985 – Keith's daughter Theodora Dupree is born,
named for Keith's grandpa Gus Dupree.

July 1985 – Live Aid; performs with Bob Dylan and Ron Wood.
They get drunk, Bob changes things at last minute, and the outcome is the worst live performance in television history by three

people who should have known better. Ron Wood: "We came off looking like real idiots."

December 12, 1985 – Death of Ian Stewart
from massive heart attack at age forty-seven. It's a terrible blow to Keith. "Who's gonna tell us off now when we misbehave?"

1986 – Produces Aretha Franklin's "Jumpin' Jack Flash."

1986 – Rumors surface of more serious tensions between Brenda and Keith.

January 23, 1986, Keith inducts Chuck Berry into the Rock and Roll Hall of Fame,
and gets away without a black eye or a lit match thrown down his shirt.

March 1986 – Release of album *Dirty Work*,
created during the peak of World War III. With Brenda gone much of the time, it's mainly a Keith-written album. Due to absence and indifference of band during recording, Keith says it was recorded by the Biff Hitler Trio. Songs include the anti-Brenda "Had It with You."

June 28, 1986 – Keith's daughter Alexandra Nicole is born.

October 1986 – Another Chuck Berry disaster.
Keith performs at his hero's sixtieth birthday concert and helps produce the film documenting the event, but it doesn't go smoothly. Berry keeps calling Keith "Jack," has repeated verbal run-ins with him, and generally creates a headache to outdo any Jagger could give.

March 1987 – Keith and Mick duke it out through the London tabloids.
It's *The Daily Mirror* (Mick) vs. *The Sun* (Keith). Keith: "He should stop trying to be like Peter Pan and grow up. I didn't change but he did. He became obsessed with age. I don't see the point of pretending that you are twenty-five when you are not. He has told me to my

face that he cannot work with me, but he cannot say why. I don't think he knows himself."

July 1987 – Signs solo deal with Virgin Records.

September 11, 1987 – Peter Tosh is murdered.
The Jamaican reggae artist signed by Rolling Stones Records was Keith's protégé. He was also a Keith headache. At one point, Tosh refused to leave Keith's house, saying Keith would need a gun to get him out. Keith eventually showed up with a machete. In the end, though, someone else did Tosh in.

January 1988 – Keith becomes Brenda.
As World War III intensifies, some insiders notice Keith and Brenda have taken on bits of each other's personalities. Keith is more "fey and camp," Brenda more "human and earthy."

May 18, 1988 – Reported meeting between Keith and Brenda
at London's Savoy Hotel to salvage the relationship. Keith tells Brenda: "Listen, darling, this thing is bigger than both of us."

October 1988 – *Talk Is Cheap* is released.
With this first solo record, Keith gives a screw-you to Brenda. On December 15 he takes the screw-you live: *Keith Richards and the X-Pensive Winos Live at the Hollywood Palladium.* The album, which many reviewers refer to as being the best Stones album in years, includes the anti-Brenda song "You Don't Move Me."

1989 – World War III comes to a close in Barbados.
Keith and Brenda are back at work together again, laughing about what they called each other in the press, and quickly get down a string of songs.

January 18, 1989 – Rock and Roll Hall of Fame induction.
Pete Townshend introduces them with the compliment, "Whatever you do, don't grow old gracefully. It wouldn't suit you."

August 1, 1989 – *Steel Wheels* is released,

includes songs "Mixed Emotions" and Keith's "Slipping Away." Steel Wheels tour begins in the U.S.

1990s – MORE TROUBLE. WHAT ELSE?

May 1990 – Urban Jungle tour.

July 1990 – Keith's finger is punctured and infected.

Concerts are delayed. Luckily, finger is insured for $1.6 million. More Stones catastrophe soon ensues, when, four months later, Keith Jr., aka Ron Wood, breaks both legs in a traffic accident. No specific insurance there, however.

April 1, 1991 – *Flashpoint*, another live album, is released, but otherwise it's a dud year.

"The Stones have got too big ... they work on a gigantic scale and you're either doing that or you're doing nothing for two years."

October 1992 – Second solo album, *Main Offender* is released,

includes reggae-inspired "Words of Wonder." The original album title is *Blame Hound*.

January 1993 – Bill Wyman leaves the Stones; Keith does not take it in stride.

"I thought of making him play at gunpoint."

"How dare you? Nobody leaves."

"It was a huge surprise when he actually said, 'I'm going to leave the group.' Nobody says that—that's a kind of *Spinal Tap* line."

July 19, 1994 – *Voodoo Lounge* is released.

Title attributed to stray kitten Keith took into his house and named Voodoo, and the area Keith created for him called Voodoo's Lounge. Songs include Keith's "Thru and Thru" and "The Worst." Voodoo Lounge tour follows.

October 1994 – Son Marlon marries model Lucie de la Falaise,
from family of Yves Saint Laurent's muse Lou Lou de la Falaise.

1996 – The public sees a rare side of Keith with *At Home with Books*,
a coffee-table book about great home libraries and their collectors,
which includes a chapter on Keith's lair.

May 1996 – Keith's granddaughter Ella Rose is born to son Marlon.

1997 – Feud begins with Elton John.
Keith says Elton only writes songs for dead blondes. True enough.
Elton says Keith looks like a monkey with arthritis. That's low.

September 23, 1997 – *Bridges to Babylon* is released,
includes Keith's reggae-inspired "You Don't Have to Mean It,"
"Low Down," and "Thief in the Night." Plus: the accidentally stolen "Anybody Seen My Baby?" (from k.d. lang's "Constant Craving").

October 1997 – *Wingless Angels* is released.
Keith's recording of Justin Hinds's drumming collective at his Jamaica
home; it was produced through Keith's newly formed Mindless Records.

April 1998 – Keith Jr., aka Ron Wood,
doing his part for the disaster routine, inadvertently has his boat
explode off the coast of Brazil.

May 18, 1998 – Broken ribs and a punctured lung.
Keith falls off a ladder at his home library in Connecticut when he
reaches for a book on Leonardo da Vinci and ends up under a pile
of encyclopedias.

August 1998 – Daughter Angela marries.
She works with horses and marries a carpenter. Keith performs at
the wedding.

1999 – The man known as being on the permanent night shift now gets up at seven A.M.

"After a few months, I was allowed to drive the kids to school. Then I was allowed to take the garbage out."

2000s – MORE TROUBLE AHEAD, AND THIS TIME IT'S PERSONAL.

August 30, 2000 – Father, Bert, dies at age eighty-five.

In his final moments, he gives Keith a wink. After having been estranged for twenty years, they developed a strong bond, with regular games of dominoes, meals of bangers and mash, and Bert coming to concerts.

Summer 2000 – Keith's grandson Orson Richards is born to son Marlon.

2001 – Assists on religious recording of Lutheran singer (and sister-in-law) Marsha Hansen; records with Sheryl Crow; performs at the Beacon Theatre for the Rainforest Alliance.

October 20, 2001 – Performs with Mick at the Concert for New York City at Madison Square Garden in honor of 9/11's firemen and police.

"Cops and firemen, they're some of our biggest fans. If I'm walking in New York City and it's [raining], they say, 'Hey, Keith, wanna lift?' "

December 2001 – *"Dogshit" in the Doorway* is released

(Keith's name for Mick's new solo album, *Goddess in the Doorway*).

December 7, 2001 – At *Gosford Park* movie premiere in New York, Keith's limo is surrounded by armed guards, as it is believed to be a stolen vehicle.

September 3, 2002 – Forty Licks World Tour opens in Boston.

October 2002 – Johnny Depp channels Keith as pirate Jack Sparrow in *Pirates of the Caribbean*, which begins filming.

At first, Disney executives freak out—they can't figure out who or what Depp's trying to be. Worries are later dispelled when film breaks box-office records, reviews are enthusiastic, and Jack Sparrow finds stardom in pop culture. Word gets around just who Depp is imitating.

March 2003 – Keith has a tantrum onstage in Osaka, Japan,

and charges at Mick twice in a full rage in what looks like an attempt to push him off the stage.

June 2003 – *Pirates of the Caribbean* premieres.

Roger Ebert writes: "There has never been a pirate, or for that matter a human being, like this."

December 12, 2003 – Brenda becomes Her Majesty.

Brenda (née Mick) Jagger is knighted "for Services to Music in the Queen's Birthday Honours." Keith is not amused. He now refers to Mick as "Her Majesty." "I don't want to step out onstage with someone wearing a fucking coronet and sporting the old ermine … It's a fucking paltry honor. If you're into this shit, hang on for the peerage. Don't settle for a little badge." Her Majesty's response: "He's like a bawling child who hasn't got an ice cream. It's nothing new. Keith likes to make a fuss."

May 2004 – Duet with Willie Nelson, "We Had It All," in Los Angeles.

A few weeks later, Keith performs at a neighborhood club in his adopted hometown in Connecticut.

June 2004 – First mortality scare in the Rolling Stones that doesn't involve Keith.

Charlie Watts is diagnosed with throat cancer.

February 2005 – The Stones play Super Bowl halftime.

Keith says he'll use offstage time to watch tennis.

September 5–6, 2005 – *A Bigger Bang* is released.

Songs include anti-Bush "Neo-con," which Keith objects to, claiming it was Mick's idea ("I live here, he doesn't"). The Keith tracks are "Infamy" and "This Place Is Empty."

April 27, 2006 – Keith falls out of a "coconut tree."

As quickly as the story starts, the story morphs. First, he was alone. Next, he was up there with Ronnie. First it's a tree, then it's a bush. Whatever it was, Keith fell out of it. There's brain surgery, trepanning. The story morphs some more: There was a jet-ski crash as well. Keith recovers and posts a laughing "I'm still here" on his Web site. Doctors are amazed by his good health. Rumors start that medical professionals are vying for his remains to study his longevity.

October 29, 2006 – Longtime Stones associate, record executive Ahmet Ertegun, falls backstage

at a concert, goes into a coma for almost two months, then dies on December 14.

November 2006 – Arkansas Governor Mike Huckabee offers to intervene between Keith and God.

He formally issues a pardon for the 1975 reckless-driving ticket and tells *GQ*: "Now that I've pardoned Keith Richards, wouldn't it be incredible if that somehow led to my being able to give him a full pardon before God for all the things he's done?"

April 2007 – "Keith Richards Snorted Father's Ashes."

The bit appears in a *New Music Express* interview, and the resulting media attention is explosive. Keith quickly recants the story, then recants the recant, claiming he didn't want to upset his dying mother.

April 21, 2007 – Death of mother, Doris Richards, at age ninety-one.

May 2007 – Look out, Mickey Mouse.

Keith appears as Captain Teague, the father of Johnny Depp's Captain Jack Sparrow, in Disney's *Pirates of the Caribbean: At World's End*.

July 2007 – Sells his memoirs for a reported $7.3 million.

August 2007 – Writes angry letter to the editor of a Swedish newspaper,

addressing a critic who panned Keith's drunken performance. He demands an apology and orders them to "write the truth." It doesn't happen.

August 26, 2007 – Eats cigarette onstage in London.

February 2008 – Martin Scorsese's concert film *Shine a Light* premieres at the Berlin Film Festival.

Afterward, Keith is reportedly "arrested" again at Newark Airport due to a passport "misunderstanding."

March 2008 – At age sixty-four, Keith becomes a fashion model.

He appears in an ad for luxury leather company Louis Vuitton and their "core values" campaign. The slogan: "Some journeys cannot be put into words." Fashion model's payment goes to Al Gore's environmental initiative.

November 2008 – Next stop: easy listening?

After a few tracks leak onto the Internet of Keith singing gentle oldies, rumors surface that he has ideas to record an easy listening album, featuring renditions of Judy Garland and Perry Como songs.

In Closing:
A RECIPE FOR
SHEPHERD'S PIE

This is a dish that has long been a Keith favorite and the standard Keith Richards meal provided on tours. One that you don't mess with. A favorite rumor is that he pulled a gun on a roadie who tried to take a bite when he thought no one was looking.

But beyond the guns, or at least the rumored threats of guns, shepherd's pie is basically Keith Richards in epicurean form: down to earth, unpretentious, natural, easy, authentic.

But be warned: if you're not careful, and take it on as something outside of your limits—for example, if you use tainted lamb, or if you are allergic to potatoes or milk, or you eat seventeen servings in a row, or take a bite from the stash of the wrong person—it can kill you.

So before you eat it, be sure you know yourself.

Keith's Mum's Shepherd's Pie Recipe*

"The one food I can eat 365 days a year."

INGREDIENTS

3 pounds of potatoes, peeled, diced

1 tablespoon of butter

Salt and pepper to taste

2 pounds ground beef

2 large onions, chopped

2 large carrots, grated

1 12-ounce can of beef stock

1 tablespoon of corn starch

Place potatoes in a large saucepan, cover with water. Bring to a boil, reduce heat, and simmer until tender. Drain. Using an electric mixer or whisk, mash potatoes and butter. Season with salt and pepper. Set aside.

Heat a large skillet. Add beef and onions. Season with salt and pepper. Add carrots and beef stock. Mix in corn starch and cook ten minutes. Pour into pie dish and top with mashed potatoes. Place under broiler until potatoes begin to turn brown.

Makes 6 servings

Note: Shepherd's pie can be made with either beef or lamb, although as a beef dish it is also referred to as cottage pie. Grated cheese is optional but should definitely be left out of Keith's pie, considering it is the one thing he will never put in his body.

* Reproduced by permission from Wendy Diamond, *A Musical Feast: Recipes from over 100 of the World's Most Famous Musical Artists* (New York: Global Liaisons, Incorporated, 1995), 83.

ACKNOWLEDGMENTS

Many thanks to the following:

At Writers House: Dan Lazar and Steven Malk

At Bloomsbury USA: Benjamin Adams and Colin Dickerman

And at both companies: Stephen Barr, Lindsay Davis, Josh Getzler, Will Georgantas, Carrie Majer, Jenny Miyasaki, Maja Nikolic, and Gena Smith

Plus, beyond: Nick Carbo, Jack Chernos, Marcy Dermansky, Anita Fore, Michael Gross, Aimee Laberge, Anne LeClaire, The Leos, Seymour Lerner, Caroline Caz Pittet, Tami and Raia Pallington, Barbara and Kenneth A. Pfeil, and Mary Ellen Sanger

REFERENCES

The quotations from Keith Richards that appear throughout the book come from a wide variety of sources and more than four decades of media. Some pieces provided more material than others, particularly the *Rolling Stone* interviews, and interviews in *Uncut*, *New Music Express*, *Mojo*, *Raygun*, *Vanity Fair*, *GQ*, *Esquire*, *Guitar World*, and *Guitar Player*. The interviewers in these publications had a talent for drawing out great lines from Keith on many different subjects.

An important video source was the documentary *25×5: The Continuing Adventures of the Rolling Stones*. The six biographies referenced (by Barbara Charone, Alan Clayson, Kris Needs, Victor Bockris, Stanley Booth, and Christopher Sandford) all provided an excellent overview of Keith's life. The Booth and Bockris biographies provided a particularly rich source of quotations.

Significant sources were the interviews conducted by Jas Obrecht and his associates for *Guitar Player* in the early 1990s, then printed over the next several years in that publication as well as others.

Books

Appleford, Steve. *The Rolling Stones: Rip This Joint: The Stories Behind Every Song.* Cambridge, MA: DaCapo Press, 2001.

Berry, Chuck. *The Autobiography.* New York: Harmony Books, 1987.

Blake, Mark. *Stone Me.* London: Aurum Press, 2008.

Bockris, Victor. *Keith Richards: The Biography.* New York: Poseidon Press, 1992.

Bonnano, M. *The Rolling Stones Chronicle.* London: Plexus, 1995.

Booth, Stanley. *Dance with the Devil: The Rolling Stones and Their Times (aka The True Adventures of the Rolling Stones)*, New York: Random House, 1984.

———. *Keith: Standing in the Shadows.* New York: St. Martin's Press, 1995.

Charone, Barbara. *Keith Richards: Life As a Rolling Stone.* Garden City, NY: Dolphin/Doubleday, 1982.

Clayson, Alan. *Keith Richards.* London: Sanctuary Publishing Ltd., 2004.

———. *The Rolling Stones: The Origin of the Species.* Surrey, England: Chrome Dreams, 2007.

Cooper, Michael, with Terry Southern and Keith Richards. *The Early Stones.* New York: Hyperion, 1992.

Dalton, David. *Rolling Stones in Their Own Words.* New York: Putnam, 1983.

———. *The Rolling Stones: The First Twenty Years.* New York: Alfred A. Knopf, 1981.

Davis, Stephen. *Old Gods Almost Dead*. New York: Broadway Books, 2001.

Diamond, Wendy. *A Musical Feast: Recipes from over 100 of the World's Most Famous Musical Artists*. New York: Global Liasons, Incorporated, 1995.

Egan, Sean. *The Rough Guide to the Rolling Stones*. New York: Rough Guides, 2006.

Epting, Chris. *Led Zeppelin Crashed Here: The Rock and Roll Landmarks of North America*. Santa Monica: Santa Monica Press, 2007.

Editors of *Esquire*. *Esquire: The Meaning of Life: Wit, Wisdom, and Wonder from 65 Extraordinary People*. New York: Hearst Books, 2004.

Ewing, Jon. *Quote Unquote: The Rolling Stones*. New York: Random House, 1996.

Faithfull, Marianne, and David Dalton. *Faithfull*. New York: Little, Brown, 1994.

Flippo, Chet. *On the Road with the Rolling Stones: Twenty Years of Lipstick, Handcuffs, and Chemicals*. New York: Doubleday, 1985.

Frankl, Viktor E. *Man's Search for Meaning*. Boston: Beacon Press, 1959.

Giuliano, Geoffrey. *The Rolling Stones Album: Thirty Years of Music and Memorabilia*. New York: Studio Books, 1993.

Gordon, Robert, and Keith Richards (foreword). *Can't Be Satisfied: The Life and Times of Muddy Waters*. New York: Little, Brown, 2002.

Gracian, Baltasar. *The Art of Worldly Wisdom*. Boston: Shambhala, 1993.

Gray, Michael. *The Bob Dylan Encyclopedia*. New York: Continuum International Publishing Group, 2005.

Greenfield, Robert. *Exile on Main Street*. Cambridge, MA: Da Capo Press, 2006.

Holland, Jools, and Dara Lowenstein. *The Rolling Stones: A Life on the Road*. New York: Penguin Studio, 1998.

Hotchner, A.E. *Blown Away: The Rolling Stones and the Death of the Sixties*. New York: Simon and Schuster, 1990.

Karnbach, James, and Carol Bernson. *It's Only Rock 'n' Roll: The Ultimate Guide to the Rolling Stones*. New York: Facts on File, 1997.

Magee, Bryan. *The Story of Philosophy*. New York: DK Publishing, Inc., 1998.

Moser, Margaret, and Bill Crawford. *Rock Stars Do the Dumbest Things*. Los Angeles: Renaissance Books, 1998.

Needs, Kris. *Keith Richards: Before They Make Me Run*. London: Plexus, 2004.

Norman, Philip. *The Stones*. London: Elm Tree Books/Hamish Hamilton, 1984.

Oldham, Andrew Loog. *Stoned: A Memoir of London in the 1960s*. New York: St. Martin's Press, 2001.

Palmer, Robert. *The Rolling Stones*. Garden City, NY: Doubleday, 1983.

Paytress, Mark. *The Rolling Stones Files*. Surrey, UK: CLB, 1995.

———. *The Rolling Stones: Off the Record*. London: Omnibus Press, 2003.

Pine-Coffin, R.S. (trans.). *The Confessions of Saint Augustine*. New York: Penguin Books, 1961.

Rolling Stones, The (Mick Jagger, Keith Richards, Charlie Watts, and Ronnie Wood) with Dara Lowenstein and Philip Dodd (editors). *According to the Rolling Stones*. San Francisco: Chronicle, 2003.

Sandford, Christopher. *Keith Richards: Satisfaction*. New York: Carroll & Graf, 2003.

Sandison, David, and Allan Jones. *Rock 'n' Roll People*. London: Hamlyn, 2000.

St. Michel, Mick. *Keith Richards in His Own Words*. London: Omnibus, 1994.

Tibballs, Geoff. *The Mammoth Book of Zingers, Quips, and One Liners*. New York: Carroll & Graf, 2004.

Wells, Simon. *The Rolling Stones: 365 Days*. New York: Abrams, 2006.

White, Timothy. *Rock Lives*. New York: Henry Holt, 1990.

Wood, Ron. *Ronnie*. New York: St. Martin's Press, 2007.

Wyman, Bill. *Rolling with the Stones*. New York: DK Publishing, 2002.
Wyman, Bill with Ray Coleman. *Stone Alone*. New York: Viking, 1990.

Magazines

Ali, Lorraine. "Satisfaction Guaranteed." *Newsweek* (August 15, 2005).
Altman, Billy. "Blood from a Stone." *Entertainment Weekly* (November 6, 1992).
Appleyard, Bryan. "Keith Rolls On." *Vanity Fair* (December 1992).
Beaumont, Mark. Keith Richards interview. *New Music Express* (April 2007).
Bockris, Victor. "Interview: Keith Richard." *High Times* (January 1978).
Bonici, Ray. "Keith Richards: Absolutely Alfalfa." *Creem* (January 1982).
Booth, Stanley. "Keith Richards Interview." *Playboy* (October 1989).
Bosso, Joseph. "Keith! Tunings, Tele, and the Cosmic Shuffle." *Guitar World* (December 1988).
Botbol, Michel. "Meet the Family." *Harper's Bazaar* (June 2000).
Browne, David. "Glimmer of Youth." *Entertainment Weekly* (October 3, 1997).
Carr, Roy. "The Keith Richard Interview." *Creem* (December 1978).
Charone, Barbara. "Keith Richards." *Creem* (June 1977).
———. "Keith Richards: Exile on the 32ⁿᵈ Floor." *Sounds* (April 2, 1977).
Cohen, Rich. "It's Show Time." *Rolling Stone* (August 25, 1994).
DeCurtis, Anthony. "Keith Richards: The Interview." *Rolling Stone* (October 6, 1988).
———. "The Making of (I Can't Get No) Satisfaction." *Rolling Stone* (July 2–23, 1998).
Deevoy, Adrian. "Persona Non Grata." *Q* (October 1988).
———. "Ladies and Gentlemen, the Interesting Old Farts." *Q* (August 1994).
Di Perna, Alan. "Keith Richards Comes Clean." (October 1997).
———. "Heart of Stone," (reprinted from *Guitar World*, October 2002), *Guitar Legends*.
———. "Back with a Bang." *Guitar World* (November 2005).
Doerschuk, Robert. *Musician* (November 1997).
Doyle, Tom. "Keith Richards: the Mojo Interview." *Mojo* (September 2007).
Ehrlich, Dimitri. "Keith Richards." *Interview* (December 2002–January 2003).
Fricke, David. "The Rhythm Twins." *Rolling Stone* (September 4, 1997).
———. "People of the Year: Mick Jagger and Keith Richards." *Rolling Stone* (December 12, 2002).
———. "Dancing with Mr. D: Keith Richards." *Rolling Stone* (October 17, 2002).
———. "Online Exclusive: Keith Richards: Uncut." *Rollingstone.com* (September 24, 2002).
———. "Back with a Band." *Rolling Stone* (September 22, 2005).
———. "Blues Brothers." *Rolling Stone* (April 17, 2008).
Garbarini, Vic. "Keith Richards: The Heart of the Stones." *Musician* (December 1983).
German, Bill. "A Stone Unturned." *Spin* (October 1985).
Graf, Gary. "The Naked Truth" (reprinted from *Guitar World*, February 1996), *Guitar Legends*.
Greenfield, Robert. "Keith Richards: The Rolling Stone Interview." *Rolling Stone* (August 19, 1971).
Hagety, Neil, and Jennifer Herrema. "Keith Richards Interview." *Raygun* 22 (January 22, 1995).
Hainey, Michael. "The GQ&A: Keith Richards." *GQ* online (menstyle.com, 2008).
Heath, Chris. "Keith Richards." *Rolling Stone* (December 25, 1997–January 8, 1998).
———. "Notes from the Babylon Bar." *Rolling Stone* (December 11, 1997).
Hofacker, Ernst. (Title not specified.) *Musik Express* (October 26, 1988).
Hoskyns, Barney. "Keith Richards: How Do You Stop?" *Mojo* (November 1997).

Hoskyns, Barney. "Keith Richards: Talk is Cheap." *Mojo* (May 1997).

Johnson, Brian. "The Stones at 50." *Macleans* (February 15, 1993).

Kutina, Scott E. "Keith Richard." *Guitar Player* (November 1977).

Loder, Kurt. "Keith Richards: The Rolling Stone Interview." *Rolling Stone* (November 12, 1981).

——. "Keith Richards." *Rolling Stone* (November 5–December 10, 1987).

——. "Keith Richards." *Rolling Stone* (October 6, 1988).

——. "Keith Richards." *Rolling Stone* (October 15, 1992).

——. "Keith Richards." (May 3–17, 2007, Fortieth Anniversary Issue).

McInerney, Jay. "The Rebel Yells." *GQ* (April 2003).

Milkowski, Bill. "Keith Richards: Wait'll Mick Hears This." *Pulse!* (October 1988).

Mueller, Andrew. "Mick's a Maniac: Interview with Keith Richards." *Uncut* (April 2008).

Neely, Kim. "Keith: Rock's Main Offender." *Rolling Stone* (November 26, 1992).

Nelson, Paul. "Keith Richads." *Circus* (September 29, 1977).

Osbrecht, Jas. "Keith Richards: Filthy, Filthy, Filthy!" *Guitar Player* (December 1992).

Petreycik, Rick. "Keith Richards." *Penthouse* (February 1996).

Richardson, John H. "What I've Learned: Keith Richards." Esquire.com (October 31, 2005).

Robbins, Ira. "Stone Wino Rhythm Guitar God Keith Richards Can Still Rip It Up." *Pulse!* (November 1992).

Santoro, Gene. "The Mojo Man Rocks Out—Keith Richards: The Guitar World Interview" (reprinted from *Guitar World*, March 1986). *Guitar Legends*.

Schoemer, Karen. "Keith Richards: Stone Icon, Rock Survivor." *New York Times* (October 18, 1992).

Sheffield, Rob. "The Rolling Stones." *Rolling Stone* (September 22, 2005).

Snow, Mat. "Keith Richards." *Q* (November 1992).

——. "Keith Richards: An English Werewolf in London." *New Music Express* (February 1986).

Spedding, Chris. "Keith on Keeping On." *Details* (April 1986).

Susman, Gary. "Beggar's Banquet." *Ew.com* (December 12, 2003).

Sweeting, Adam. "Keith Richards." *Uncut* (December 2002).

Welsh, Chris. "An Outlaw at the Ritz: Keith Richards." *Melody Maker* (January 1979).

Wheeler, Tom. "Keith Richards." *Guitar Player* (April 1983).

——. "Keith Richards: Not Fade Away." *Guitar Player* (December 1989).

Wild, David. "Blood Brothers." *Rolling Stone* (May 31, 2007).

Wilde, Jon and Nigel Williamson. "Keith Richards 60th Birthday Special." *Uncut* (January 2004).

Young, Charles M. "Keith Richards' Revenge." *Musician Magazine* (October 1988).

"Keith Richards." *Creem* (February 1982).

Entertainment Weekly (May 28, 1999).

"What Rock 'n' Roll Has Taught Me: Keith Richards." *New Music Express* (April 7, 2007).

Newsweek (October 24, 1988).

People (November 9, 1992).

People (August 11, 1986).

Q (October 1987).

Rolling Stone (July 6, 1972).

Rolling Stone (August 3, 1972).

Rolling Stone (February 4, 1993).

"The Rolling Stones: Out for Blood." *Rolling Stone* (August 24, 1994).
Spin (January 1993).
"Keith Richards." *Vanity Fair* (January 2003).
Zigzag (November 1980).

Newspapers

Armstrong, Lisa. "Keith Richards: My Life in Fashion." *The Times* (April 23, 2008).
Boston Globe (October 10, 1997).
Christensen, Thor. "When I'm 64." *Dallas Morning News* (posted online: October 30, 2008).
Daily Telegraph (January 2, 2008).
Guardian (December 5, 2003).
Gunderson, Edna. "They Sing to Their Dad's Tunes." *USA Today* (June 14, 1997).
———. "The Stones Take the Road in Their Fifth Decade." *USA Today* (September 10, 2002).
———. "Four Rockers Define Stones Age." *USA Today* (August 2005).
Hoskyns, Barney. "Keith Richards." *Independent* (June 1999).
Harrington, Richard. "Keith Richards: Old Man Riffer." *Washington Post* (October 19, 1997).
Independent on Sunday (August 7, 1994).
McNair, James. "Keith Richards: Being Keef." *Independent* (August 2, 2005).
New York Times (April 7, 2007).
Orange County Register (August 8, 1986).
Schechter, Harold. "Mourning on the Inside." *New York Times* (June 4, 1989).
Shedden, Iain. "Still Rolling As Years Go By." *Australian* (February 18, 2003).
Spectator (November 15, 2003).
Spitz, Bob. "Raw, Raunchy, and Middle Aged: Rolling Stone Keith Richards at 45." *The New York Times* (June 4, 1989).
Sunday Times (August 17, 2003).
Sunday Times (December 2, 2003).
Winnipeg Free Press (October 31, 2007).

Film, Video, and Television

25x5: The Continuing Adventures of the Rolling Stones. Directed by Nigel Finch. CBS Music Video, 1990.
Cocksucker Blues. Directed by Robert Frank and Daniel Seymour. Unreleased, 1972.
Gimme Shelter. Directed by David Maysles, Albert Maysles, Charlotte Zwerin. Maysles Films Inc., 1970.
Gram Parsons: Fallen Angel. Directed by Gandulf Hennig. BBC Music, 2004.
Hail! Hail! Rock 'n' Roll. Directed by Taylor Hackford. Universal Pictures, 1987.
Keith Richards: Under Review. Directed by Tom O'Dell. ChromeDreams, 2007.
Muddy Waters: Can't be Satisfied. Directed by Morgan Neville and Robert Gordon. Winstar, 2003.
The Real Buddy Holly Story. Produced by Paul McCartney. White Star, 1984.
The Rolling Stones: Just for the Record. Directed by Steven Vosburgh. Passport Video, 2002.
The Rolling Stones: Satisfaction: Interviews. Music Video Distributors, 2007.
Shine a Light. Directed by Martin Scorsese. Paramount, 2008.
Keith Richards, "Induction ceremony for The Ronettes." Rock and Roll Hall of Fame, Waldorf-Astoria Hotel, New York. March 12, 2007.

"The Stones: Still Rocking, Still Controversial." *BBC Newsnight*. Interviewed by Robin Denselow. September 2005.

"Mick Jagger and Keith Richards Still on a Roll." *The Today Show*. Interviewed by Matt Lauer. May 16, 2005.

Radio

Rockline Radio Interview with Keith Richards (June 19, 1992).

Nicky Campbell Interview, BBC Radio (December 26, 1995).

CDs

Loose Talk (interview compilation). Delta, 1996.

Needs, Kris. *Keith Richards: The Classic Interview*. ChromeDreams, 2006.

Other

Langsam, David (1988). "The Politics, Philosophy and Psychology of the Rolling Stones." An interview with Keith Richards. (Unknown original source; posted on http://ourworld.compuserve.com/homepages/dingonet/keithric.htm)

Web Sites Consulted

Angelfire.com; Bigpicture.fancast.com; Bitchycelebrity.com; Brainyquote.com; Contactmusic.com; EverythingKeith.com; Ew.com; Fancast.com; Hiphopelements.com; Inform.com; IORR.org; Irelandonline.com; Keithrichards.com; Monstersandcritics.com; News.BBC.UK; Quotationspage.com; Pierresetparoles .blogspot.com; Reuters.com; Rocksbackpages.com; Rollingstone.com; Rollingstones .com; Rollingstones.org; Thinkexist.com; Timeisonourside.com; Timesonline.co.uk; Washingtonpost.com; Wikiquote.org; World-of-Keith-Richards.piczo.com.

Youtube Videos

Due to the minimal background usually provided by those who upload videos, it is not possible to create a comprehensive source list of material found on YouTube .com; even URLs are not reliable, since clips come and go. However, the following key words and phrases (along with the term "Keith Richards," of course) may unearth a number of pertinent interviews with Keith.

"1 to One, VH1: Keith Richards in Jamaica with Anthony DeCurtis"; "2DF 2006 interview"; "*20/20*. ABC-TV, Rolling Stones Interview 1989"; "British TV interview 1974: Old Grey Whistle Test"; "British TV interview 2007"; "Chicago 1992"; "Dutch TV interview"; "Dutch TV interview 2005"; "Finnish TV interview 1988"; "French TV interview 1988"; "Keith Richards Interview from 1973"; "Interview from 1977"; "Interview from 1982"; "Keith Richards Interview 1992"; "Keith Richards Interview in 1988"; "Keith Richards Interviewed by Hunter S. Thompson, *ABC In Concert*, ABC Television" aka "Hunter meets Keith"; "Madrid interview 1982"; "Making of 'Pirates of the Caribbean' with Johnny Depp and Keith Richards"; "Mexican TV interview 2005"; "Mick and Keith-Rolling Stones-Documentary 1998-Swedish TV"; "Keith Richards: Music is Stronger than That"; "Newsnight June 24, 1982 and 2005"; "Philippe Manoeuvre Interview"; "Rolling Stones Emotional Rescue Release Party, 1980 in New York"; "The Rolling Stones in Morocco, BBC Television, 1989"; "The Rolling Stones interviews on *Sixty Minutes*, CBS-TV, with Ed Bradley"; "Shanghai Interview, CNN, 2006"; "TFI Friday 1999 with Chris Evans, UK TV"; "Youtube Living Legends interview, with Mick and Keith."

A NOTE ON THE AUTHOR

Like most die-hard Stones fans, Jessica Pallington West has had a fascination with "the World's Greatest Rock 'n' Roll Band" that has taken on near-religious proportions.

She is the author of a book on another obsession, *Lipstick*, and her writing has been featured in magazines, newspapers, radio, TV, and the Web, including About.com, Neiman Marcus's *The Book*, the *Daily Telegraph*, BBC Television, and BBC Radio.

She has received fellowships from the Virginia Center for the Creative Arts, and from the Ucross, Ragdale, and Helene Wurlitzer foundations

She was the sole adult member of an otherwise all-children's rock band, consisting of a bunch of pipsqueak toughs influenced by the Stones.